Llewellyn's
2017
Witches'
Companion

An Almanac for Everyday Living

Llewellyn's 2017 Witches' Companion

ISBN 978-0-7387-3766-9

Art Director: Lynne Menturweck
Cover art © Tim Foley
Cover designer: Lynne Menturweck
Designer: Joanna Willis
Editor: Andrea Neff

Interior illustrations:
Neil Brigham: 53, 55, 56, 58, 61, 108, 110, 113, 225, 227
Kathleen Edwards: 11, 13, 15, 18, 89, 92, 125, 127, 129, 159, 162, 207, 210, 257, 260
Tim Foley: 9, 33, 35, 37, 40, 85, 95, 97, 101, 104, 139, 142, 145, 167, 171, 175, 200, 203, 213, 0248, 253
Bri Hermanson: 43, 48, 50, 133, 137, 192, 194, 197, 239, 242, 245
Jennifer Hewitson: 23, 26, 29, 75, 77, 80, 83, 116, 121, 150, 154, 215, 216, 220, 265, 266, 269
Rik Olson: 66, 69, 70, 179, 182, 186, 231, 233, 236

Additional illustrations: Llewellyn Art Department

Any Internet references contained in this work are current at publication time, but the publisher cannot guarantee that a specific location will continue to be maintained.

You can order Llewellyn annuals and books from New Worlds, Llewellyn's magazine catalog. To request a free copy of the catalog, call toll-free 1-877-NEW-WRLD or visit our website at http://www.llewellyn.com.

Llewellyn Worldwide Ltd.
2143 Wooddale Drive
Woodbury, MN 55125-2989
www.llewellyn.com

Printed in the United States of America

Contents

Community Forum

Provocative Opinions on Contemporary Topics

Witchy Living

Day-by-Day Witchcraft

Witchcraft Essentials

Practices, Rituals & Spells

Magical Transformations

Everything Old Is New Again

The Lunar Calendar

September 2016 to December 2017

Community Forum

PROVOCATIVE OPINIONS ON
CONTEMPORARY TOPICS

Save the Witch: Putting an End to Witchcraft Persecution Around the World

Melanie Marquis

Around the world, thousands of suspected Witches are killed each year, and many more face torture, exile, and other forms of extreme abuse. While the idea of Witches being burned alive, hung, stoned, or tortured is widely thought of as a relic of the past, relegated to the Spanish Inquisition, the Salem witch trials, and other dark periods in human history, Witchcraft persecution pervades and persists in modern times in many places around the world, from urban America to rural regions of Africa, South America, India, Western Europe,

and the Pacific. As a local co-ordinator for the Pagan Pride Project—an organization that seeks to encourage religious tolerance and foster pride in Pagan religions through education, activism, charity, and other community efforts—I've heard many firsthand accounts of custody battles, lost jobs, inconsiderate or downright cruel treatment from family or friends, and other tales of discrimination and persecution faced by modern Witches living in the United States.

Occasionally, more extreme cases of Witchcraft persecution in America make national news. In 2014 in Queens, New York, a man was arrested for beating to death with a hammer his girlfriend and her daughter, whom he suspected of being Witches, while a 2015 murder case in Pensacola, Florida, led to accusations of Witchcraft being levied against one of the suspects by the local police department, a suspicion that was echoed by media outlets nationwide. The Pensacola incident involved the murder of an elderly lady and her two adult sons, and the investigation centered around a person of interest presumed to be Wiccan. NBC News reported the story with the headline "'Wiccan Ritual Killing' Leaves Family of Three Dead in Pensacola: Police," while the New York Post heralded the tidbit with a rather reaching "Family's Throats Slit in 'Ritualistic' Murder Tied to the Blue Moon." When questioned about the link between the murders and Witchcraft, the Pensacola sheriff responded that the nature of the injuries, the positions of the bodies, and the fact that a person of interest was known to practice Wicca led the police to suspect a connection. The police and media weren't the only ones to jump to conclusions and parade their ignorance of true Witchcraft practice. A neighbor of the victims commented, "To find out that it was this weird, satanic cult, witchcraft whatever, is just really unsettling."

However bad it might be right here in America, the situation is decidedly worse in many other places in the world. Accused Witches in Bolivia are often burned to death or buried alive, while mob killings prompted by suspicion of Witchcraft are common occurrences in Haiti, Guatemala, Papua New Guinea, Tanzania, Nigeria, Ghana, Democratic Republic of the Congo, Nepal, India, South Africa, and many other countries.

People accused of Witchcraft are often subjected to beatings, torture, stoning, burning, sexual assault, exile, and other abuses too atrocious to detail. Although Witchcraft persecution affects people from a wide range of demographics, among the most often targeted are women and children, with elderly women and children with disabilities or other differences being the most vulnerable. The abusers are rarely prosecuted, and many governments respond to the problem by enacting laws not against the murderers of suspected Witches but against the practice of Witchcraft itself.

With killings of accused Witches numbering in the thousands each year and instances of beatings, torture, and other forms of violent persecution occurring by the millions, Witch-hunting is truly a global epidemic that calls for a global solution. Underlying causes of economic and social disparity, political repression, health crises, war, dramatic ecological change, lack of education, and other contributing factors must be addressed, and governments and religious leaders alike must be petitioned to take action toward finding and implementing solutions. United Nations–sponsored educational programs meant to increase public awareness and understanding of the issue have met with success in areas of Chad and Sudan, while organizations such as the South African Pagan Rights Alliance, the Pagan Pride Project, the American Civil Liberties Union, and the Lady Liberty League continue to combat Witchcraft persecution through public education, activism, and other support efforts. While such efforts are promising, they clearly are not enough. Your help is needed, too, and as an actual Witch, there's a lot you can do in addition to supporting the efforts just mentioned. Here are a couple of spells you can use to protect the persecuted and transform the persecutors.

Spell to Protect the Persecuted

Use this spell to help protect people in danger of persecution due to suspected or actual involvement in the magickal arts. This spell can be cast at any time, though a waxing or full moon is most advantageous. Begin by selecting the target for your spell—where it should go and whom it should protect. Are you casting a spell to protect a specific person whose location is known to you? Knowing this information will give you an advantage in your spellcasting. Do you want to protect whoever needs it, wherever they might be located? Even if you don't know the exact specifics of the who and where of your spell, try focusing in as much as possible. Big, ambitious magick often fails because it's too broad, too ambiguous, and too diluted.

Targeting each act of spellwork more precisely will yield better results, as the magickal power will be more concentrated and easier to direct. You might, for example, choose to focus each spell you cast on a specific country or village where Witchcraft persecution is known to be an issue. Further, you might choose to focus on protecting children, elderly women, or another particular group of people at risk of persecution. Keep in mind that you can cast such spells as often as you're able and inclined to do so. You might focus on a different country or region each day, week, month, or season. You might get together with some friends and organize into groups, each brigade focusing on the protection of a specific person or group of people. The point is to be as specific as possible so that the magick is more effective, and to switch up your focus now and then so you can cover more territory.

Once you've decided on the target area and group or individual you're aiming to protect, you will need to create a physical symbol to represent this focus. Having a physical representation of your spell's target will help you to better concentrate and clarify your intentions during the spellcasting. To represent the people you wish to protect, you might create human figures out of clay, write descriptive

information on a piece of paper, use photographs if available, or utilize a plastic doll. Identify the person or group as specifically as possible. Even if you don't know the exact identities of the people you are aiming to protect, you can utilize whatever information you do know. Try adding inscriptions to your clay figures, dolls, or other symbols, labeling them with descriptive phrases that clearly convey the identity of those represented. For instance, you might write on a piece of paper the words "women in India accused of Witchcraft," or you might label a doll with the words "child Witch."

To represent the place of focus, you might use a photograph, a map, or a news clipping detailing a case of Witchcraft persecution in the area. You might also use an object such as a rock, herb, or manufactured product originating from the area of focus. If nothing else is available, simply write the name of the place on a piece of paper, being as specific as possible.

Place the symbols you've chosen on your altar, laying the human representation on top of or directly next to the place symbol. Surround the symbols with a circle of white candles, placing the candles at enough distance to prevent any wax from dripping down on your items. If you like, sprinkle some sage, juniper, mugwort, or another protective herb in a wider ring surrounding the circle of candles.

Focus your attention on the symbols you've placed at the center of the altar, imagining as clearly as possible the people whom you wish to protect and the area in which they are located. With this image still in mind, light the candles and envision a bright, protective orb of energy radiating around the spell's target, encasing both person and place in an impenetrable shield forged of light and love. If you like, call on the aid of protective deities or other powers to help strengthen the charm. You might summon lunar energies, earth energies, Hecate, Kwan Yin, or any other force you find fitting. Ask the chosen power to join you in protecting those who are threatened. Ask them to lend their strength and energy to your spell.

Seal the charm with an incantation. Write a verse expressing your precise intentions. You can use the following one as a basic framework, but you will need to customize it a bit so that it more precisely defines your spell's focus:

I call on the powers of love and light
To protect the threatened with unmatched might!
Keep them well and keep them safe!
Keep them hid and hold their space!
They can't be touched, they can't be harmed!
They won't be hurt, they won't be found!
With love and light, they stand their ground!
They will stay safe! Love will abound!

Finish with a statement of intention that expresses the specific parameters of your spell, mentioning who you are protecting and where they are located. For example, you might finish the spell by saying, "Elderly people in South Africa are safe from persecution!" or another phrase expressing your precise intention.

Extinguish the candles or keep watch over them as they burn down. Leave everything in place on your altar for as long as possible, saving the cleanup until you need to clear the space for your next spellcasting. If you used any toxic herbs or other dangerous ingredients, however, remember to put those away so they're safely out of reach of any children or pets.

Spell to Bind and Transform the Forces of Persecution

Use this spell to restrict the actions of those who would otherwise harm suspected Witches. Casting this magick during a waning or dark moon is most effective, but it can be successfully worked at any time. Begin by writing on a small scrap of paper names or phrases that convey the identity of the persecuting forces you are aiming to resist. You might write the specific name of an oppressive or apathetic government or tribal leader, or you might write something more general, such as "those who accuse and persecute Witches in America." Think of these persecuting forces as you write the words to describe them.

Place this paper inside a jar with a tight-fitting lid. Before you seal the jar, fill it with rainwater or water from a spring, creek, river, or ocean. Add a few marigold blossoms, a pinch of dill, a sprinkling of celery or poppy seeds, or a scattering of willow leaves, along with a generous handful of sage. You can use any variety of sage, though white sage and divine sage are the most potent. Swirl the contents of the jar counterclockwise for nine rotations, then tightly seal the lid.

Shake the jar vigorously as you envision the forces of persecution on which you're focused being bound and contained, unable to harm, and transmuting from the inside out. Imagine hearts and minds changing, hate and fear evaporating, and violence being rendered an impossible option. As you shake the jar, repeat the following incantation or write your own verse to add a personal touch to the magick:

> *You cannot hurt, you cannot harm!*
> *You cannot harm a single one!*
> *Forever changed, your heart and mind,*
> *Your hate will be your own demise!*

Leave the jar and its contents outside in a sunny place until the paper begins to disintegrate. Swirl the jar nine times counterclockwise

and give it a vigorous shake each day. When you start to see little flakes of paper breaking away from the main piece, pour out the lot and rinse the jar thoroughly so it's ready for your next spell.

Helping Is the Gateway out of Helplessness

It's tempting to feel helpless when faced with combating a worldwide problem like Witchcraft persecution, but the only way to stop feeling that way is to do what you can, helping in whatever ways you deem possible. From magickal action to social outreach to political activism, there's no limit to the work that must be done. If we are to find justice and peace for those who are called by our name, we Witches must stand together and put forth our full power toward resisting and eradicating this great evil.

We Witches must unite, and with or without outside help or intervention, we must insist on an end to the persecution of our kind. Instead of trumpeting calls of "The Burning Times: Never Again!" it's time we face facts and adopt a more realistic and relevant battle cry: "The Burning Times Must End!"

Further Reading/Resources Consulted

Calabrese, Erin. "'Wiccan Ritual Killing' Leaves Family of Three Dead in Pensacola: Police." NBCNews.com, August 4, 2015. www.nbcnews .com/news/us-news/police-wiccan-ritual-killing-leaves-three-dead -pensacola-n404256.

Horowitz, Mitch. "The Persecution of Witches, 21st-Century Style." NewYorkTimes.com, July 4, 2014. www.nytimes.com/2014/07/05 /opinion/the-persecution-of-witches-21st-century-style.html?_r=0.

Pagan Pride Project, www.paganpride.org.

Schnoebelen, Jill. "Witchcraft Allegations, Refugee Protection, and Human Rights: A Review of the Evidence." United Nations High Commisioner for Refugees, January 2009. www.unhcr.org/4981ca712.pdf.

South African Pagan Rights Alliance, www.paganrightsalliance.org.

Melanie Marquis *is the creator of the* Modern Spellcaster's Tarot *(illustrated by Scott Murphy) and the author of several books, including* A Witch's World of Magick, The Witch's Bag of Tricks, Witchy Mama *(with Emily A. Francis),* Beltane, *and* Lughnasadh. *The founder of United Witches Global Coven and a local coordinator for the Pagan Pride Project, she loves sharing magick with others and has presented workshops and rituals to audiences across the US. She lives in Denver, Colorado, and can be found online at MelanieMarquis.com.*

Illustrator: Kathleen Edwards

Living Pagan at Work

Kerri Connor

For many Pagans, living as a Pagan means living a simple and pure life. A life filled with nature, love, spirituality, and compassion. A life free of greed, hate, prejudice, and envy. It's a life of being thankful and appreciative. It's a life filled with hard work, terrific celebrations, and quiet meditations.

Some people like to keep their work and home lives completely separate, no matter what religion they practice. Others tend to make friends with the people they work with and allow those lines to blur a bit. They want to feel just as at home at work as they do when they

For years we have been told that if you are a Witch or Pagan, you need to keep quiet about it. But why? Being open about who and what you are doesn't take away your power; it actually gives you more. It shows you are strong and have pride in who you are. It gives you control over your life and who you choose to share it with.

are actually at home. There are also those people who would like to be more open at work and make new friendships, but they are afraid that if their co-workers knew the truth about them, they wouldn't be welcome, not only as friends but as coworkers as well.

For years we have been told that if you are a Witch or Pagan, you need to keep quiet about it. But why? Being open about who and what you are doesn't take away your power; it actually gives you more. It shows you are strong and have pride in who you are. It gives you control over your life and who you choose to share it with. Do you really want people who are overly judgmental about your religion and spiritual practices to be in your life in the first place? I know I don't, so I've never had too much of an issue about whether it came out at work. For years I didn't overtly advertise what I was, but if religious discussions or conversations on beliefs came up, I certainly didn't hide who I was either.

As an author of Pagan books, it would be hard for me to stay in the closet at work even if I wanted to, particularly since I work at a bookstore. It's definitely an interesting experience when a customer comes to the information counter and asks for your help in finding a book you wrote!

The first bookstore I worked at was where I came up with the idea for my first book. Each of the employees at that store was asked what genre were they most familiar with, and a running list was kept at the customer service desk. That way, when a customer needed assistance in the way of recommendations, the appropriate person could be called upon to help out. I was the "expert" for the New Age section, so I dealt with a lot of Pagan customers and helped them find what they were looking for. When the type of book many of them wanted didn't exist, a friend suggested to me that I should write it, and I did. That book, *The Pocket Spell Creator*, was written over twelve years ago, but it can still be found or ordered at bookstores today.

Though before I wrote my first book I hadn't really hidden what I was, I didn't go around broadcasting it either. Some of my family members knew, but most did not. Some of my friends knew, but most did not. Once I sold the manuscript, however, all of that changed. You can't sell a manuscript and then not answer the inevitable question that comes with announcing your good news: "What's it about?" And so, you come out.

It was pretty obvious to my coworkers that if I had knowledge about the subject matter, there was a reason why, so there was never any big "coming out" at work. Bookstores really are different from other kinds of retail stores. Most of the employees are of a liberal mind, and education is high on their list of importance. These people are, for the most part, open and nonjudgmental. Customers also want someone to assist them who actually knows

what they are talking about, so keeping quiet in a situation like this would be depriving them of the help they need. From my experience, people have the hardest time asking for help in the New Age section. They are often scared of being judged, so when I see them, I do everything I can to make them feel comfortable and help them find what they need. Even when customers bring these books to the register, the vast majority of the time they place them on the counter upside down (far more than with any other genre of book), as if they do not want others to see what they are purchasing.

After I left that bookstore, I worked at several other retail stores. Sometimes religious conversations would come up (which weren't really supposed to, of course), and since I'm not one to be shy about who I am, I would contribute my unique view to the subject at hand and therefore "come out." In my experience, I have had to do a lot of explaining about what *Pagan* is. (Since I highly value education, this explanation would include the fact that *Paganus* first referred to country dwellers, and how that has evolved into *Pagans*—those not of an Abrahamic faith.) Many people have no idea whatsoever what *Pagan* means. Many have never even heard the word, or, at the very least, pretend they haven't. While I expected that most people would know the word, I also expected that they would have a bad, invalid definition of it that involved words like *devil* and *evil*. I have found that just isn't the norm, at least not where I live.

Once I began explaining, even to some of those who didn't know the word *Pagan*, I would get questions like "Is that like Wicca?" or "Is that like the Native Americans?" Others who did know the word often responded by telling me how they have a friend who practices Wicca, though only a few had a deep understanding of what that actually meant.

What I didn't get was lectures on how I was going to go to hell or how I needed to find Jesus, or return to God, or anything like that.

I didn't get hate or intolerance or threats. The only time I have ever been confronted about my beliefs in a negative manner was from my own parents when I finally told them. They lectured me. They went to their pastor and tried to "get me help." (The pastor told my parents that people only turn to Paganism when they believe they have been hurt by the Christian God—which is far from correct.) But to come out at work? That was never an issue, no matter where I worked.

One of the jobs I held was at a popular arts and crafts chain store, a place that was actually great for buying all kinds of witchy and ritual supplies. The selection for Halloween was incredible, and many of the "decorations" could be put to use year round in a Witch's home. A common question at that store for both customers and employees alike was "What project are you working on?" While I did do some crafting projects, the majority of my purchases were for ritual or spell use or decoration. I had no problem telling my coworkers the truth. Before long, my coworkers started asking me questions about how I intended to use the things I bought in my practice. But again, these questions were posed without judgment. Curiosity? Definitely. But if anyone ever said anything judgmental about me, it was never to my face.

My current position is once again at a large chain bookstore, so I get to deal with pretty much the same type of people: open-minded and nonjudgmental. When I interviewed for the position, I told the hiring manager I was an author. She asked a few questions about my writing and was excited to have a published author joining the bookstore. It wasn't until after I had been working there for a while that I found out she was an extremely devout Christian woman, yet she never once had an issue with the type of writing I do.

At one point, I thought a coworker might also be Pagan. She wore pentagram jewelry often and one necklace that was a small

planchette. She wasn't an easy person to talk to, however. We didn't work together often, and I worked at the store for an entire year before I ever saw her smile. There were only a couple of employees she seemed to be friendly with at all, and I wasn't one of them. Since we worked together so seldom, I didn't think she even knew about me being Pagan or a writer. I would see her for a few hours a month and that was it.

I really wasn't sure if she was Pagan or not, but I decided to go ahead and ask. I thought maybe if we had this in common, it might help us get along better during those few hours we did work together. But when I asked her if she was Pagan, she told me, "I don't even know what that means. What is that?" When I started to explain it to her, she cut me off with a "no" and walked away. I admit that, with her attitude, I found it pleasing that she wasn't Pagan. I have to wonder if she knows anything about the significance of a lot of the jewelry she wears. It seems as if it is done for the shock value rather than out of respect for the symbols. There doesn't seem to be any spiritual reason for it, which, frankly, is just plain sad.

A few months after that exchange, we had a new employee start who was openly gay. He didn't try to hide it at all and spoke about his husband often. He and I hit it off right away. One day when we were having one of our numerous conversations, he told me that he had the feeling we had something in common, something he didn't think he had in common with anyone else at work. I wasn't sure what he was getting at until he showed me that he had a necklace with a pentagram tucked in his shirt. I smiled and told him we did. He said he knew it and then asked me if other people in the store knew about me. When I told him it was pretty much common knowledge, he wanted to know how people had taken the news. I explained that it hadn't seemed to make a difference to anyone. A few people didn't know too much about it, other than that there were books about Paganism in the New Age section, but those who did know what it meant didn't have a problem with it anyway.

He had been nervous about coming out of that particular closet, which I found confusing. He had no problem with people knowing he was gay and that he was married to a man (and had been for two years before it became legal nationwide), but he was worried that those same people might have an issue accepting him as someone who was Pagan. He was relieved to know he wasn't the only one at work to claim that title, and he was elated to know our coworkers didn't have issue with it to begin with. I asked him why he was scared to come out as Pagan but not afraid to come out as gay. He said that the gay community is far more supportive about coming out and demanding that their voices be heard than many Pagan communities are. Some Pagan traditions still require complete secrecy, and when things are kept secret, it ends up creating problems for a person down the road and for all Pagans in general.

It is a commonly held belief that if you keep something secret about yourself, it's because either you know it's wrong or you're ashamed of it. This then makes people think that those who hide the fact that they are a Witch or Pagan are doing so because even they know it's wrong. No matter how much you may try to convince these people otherwise, chances are they aren't going to change their minds about how they feel any more than you would change your mind if they tried to convince you that Paganism is dark and evil. Arguing with them doesn't help. The best way to change a person's mind about Paganism isn't to argue with them; it's to show them with your actions what being Pagan really is.

Also, when people hide their religious beliefs, the official number of Pagans that exist in the world gets distorted. If they aren't willing to stand up and be counted, then they simply are not counted, and people do not believe that the Pagan community is growing in number.

The gay community has been very vocal about taking a stand, being counted, and demanding equal rights, and while some individuals and groups have pushed back, quite hard at times, their community hasn't given up. This is how things change. This is how slaves were freed, how women got the vote, and how segregation was ended. None of these things changed by people hiding who they were. None of these things changed without a voice.

I know that a lot of people are against Pagans coming out at work (or any place, for that matter) out of fear that they will suffer from discrimination, but I have yet to see this happen to anyone. The fear of what *may* happen is not necessarily the same as what *will* happen. I'm well aware that in some geographical areas it may be more difficult to be Pagan, but would that be the case if all Pagans were open about who they are? Wouldn't it be better if we took the time to educate our

neighbors, family members, and coworkers so they understand that being Pagan has nothing to do with devil worship, cannibalism, or whatever other crazy notions some people have? Wouldn't it be better to teach people through example rather than fight with them?

You don't need to run around and tell everyone you meet, "Hi, I'm Pagan," but you don't need to hide it either. Let your coworkers get to know the real you. Let them know what you stand for and what is important to you. Let them see that you are a good person, not someone dark and evil. Use the opportunity to teach them. Above all, never be afraid to be yourself.

Kerri Connor *is the High Priestess of the Gathering Grove. She has written several magic books, including* Spells for Tough Times.

Illustrator: Jennifer Hewitson

Pagans and Mental Illness

Autumn Damiana

Mental health is a huge concern in today's world. With the evolution of awareness in how the body, mind, and spirit are interrelated, we are more conscious than ever of the need to address issues like stress, negative thinking, bad habits, addiction, etc. Pagans seem to intuitively understand this and nurture that connection through various techniques and practices, including prayer, meditation, ritual, and alternative medicine. Pagans are also known for being more generally accepting of those who are eccentric, odd, or otherwise on the edge of mainstream society. This means that they are also less judgmental of those who are mentally ill, right?

Wrong. I wish this were not the case, but the stigma of mental illness persists, even among Pagans. Despite the incredible advances that have been made in the psychiatric field over the past few decades, there is still fear surrounding mental illness. This topic is important to me because I myself am bipolar (also called manic depressive). I was diagnosed twenty years ago and have lived with this reality my entire adult life. For better or worse, being bipolar has shaped my identity probably more than any other factor. I have also met many other Pagans who have been diagnosed with a mental illness and, like me, have questioned how this affects them spiritually.

Mental Illness and Discrimination

The most common adult mental illnesses are depression, anxiety, schizophrenia, bipolar disorder, personality disorders, addiction, and eating disorders. (Note that most of these are labeled as disorders and *not* diseases, because a disease has a known pathology and in some cases can be cured. Tuberculosis is an excellent example of a disease.) The symptoms of these illnesses can range from mild to severe, but what they all have in common is that they are disruptive enough

to interfere with a person's ability to function on a day-to-day basis. Many of these mental health issues and their manifestations are related; one can be the catalyst for another, or symptoms may be identical in more than one type of illness, and misdiagnosis is common. Therefore, it is important to understand that screening for mental illness relies on many variables and can be difficult to ascertain even by a professional, so avoid diagnosing yourself or those around you.

With that said, this subject doesn't usually even come up unless someone discloses that they have been diagnosed with a mental disorder. This is where discrimination can come into play. There are, regrettably, plenty of Pagan groups/circles that bar entry to anyone who is in treatment (including recovery and/or therapy) or is taking psychiatric medications. However, it is important to remember that this information is submitted voluntarily by that individual. I feel that such an admission should be looked at as a positive instead of a negative: yes, this person might have a more complex mental health situation than others, but the person is honest enough to admit to it and responsible enough to seek treatment. Pagans value both honesty and responsibility, and self-improvement is always seen as an admirable pursuit. So why should this be any different for those with a mental illness?

Time, Place, and Circumstance

There are those who would say that all Pagans are crazy anyway. We live by different standards than most of the population since we easily accept belief in such things as alternative medicine, the supernatural, magic, divination, past lives, alternate planes of existence, direct communication with our gods, and so on. While some of these beliefs may be commonplace in other cultures, overall they are considered strange in ours. This is one example of why the topic of mental health is so subjective—"abnormal" psychology is determined simply as being outside of what is considered "normal," and this differs greatly from one culture to the next. Because our culture values logical reasoning and concrete scientific evidence, faith-based experiences are often regarded as symptoms of mental illness, not only among Pagans but in many other spiritual traditions as well. So how is it that we can be sure that we are *not* all crazy?

There is no definitive answer to this question, but I have noticed some similarities between people's experiences. For example, a person who is attempting to see ghosts, fairies, visions, premonitions, etc., will not be alarmed if they actually do, but instead will feel rewarded if that is the result. This is distinctly different from someone who is suffering from psychosis in which they have visual or auditory hallucinations, which can cause extreme fear, paranoia, and distress because they are unwanted. Belief in magic and the ability to cast spells can be viewed as delusions of grandeur by those who do not understand a religion in which that is an accepted reality. And I personally have stories about those around me mistaking my elevated mood and the energetic "high" that I sometimes get after ritual as the beginnings of a manic episode.

The important message here is that mental illness can only be viewed from a cultural perspective. What is the norm for one group of people may be highly unorthodox for another. However, this also provides some insight into how to do a mental health reality check. I think it is safe to say that if there is a framework in place, such as a religion, that supports a belief, behavior, or practice that might seem like a symptom of mental illness, it should be further investigated. Your experiences should not necessarily be considered "wrong" unless they could cause undue or long-term physical or psychological harm. Hearing voices in a cemetery may signal that you are clairaudient, but hearing voices that say you can fly may cause you to seriously injure yourself. For example, shamans often recount that their calling and/or initiation happened as a result of a traumatic psychological event. Vodou practitioners value possession by their gods as a sacred expression of their belief. Catholics

sometimes report positive experiences of visions and/or voices that they believe have been sent to them by God. And many cultures over the ages have valued those with unusual minds, going so far as to speculate that these individuals are holy and can more readily access the spirit realm or journey into the unknown. When viewed from this perspective, I can't help but wonder if in a different time, place, and circumstance, my mental condition might have been honored as a gift. In such a culture, I likely would have become a healer, prophet, or other religious specialist even though in my present culture I am viewed as being mentally ill.

Complications and Misunderstandings

Practicing good mental health habits can sometimes prevent disorders such as depression and anxiety from getting out of control or can at least lessen the severity of the symptoms. However, a mental health professional should always be consulted if you feel that you are suffering from a mental illness, because these almost never go away on their own and can get worse over time without treatment. Likewise, self-help and spiritually based methods of dealing with a mental health condition work remarkably well in conjunction with medical care but should not be relied on as a stand-alone remedy. You can't "magic away" a mental illness.

And yet, because of the shame associated with being diagnosed with a mental illness, there are too many people, especially in the Pagan community, who refuse to seek help. Why this is the case could be a whole article by itself, but I will sum up the major reasons as I see them. For one, the DIY spirit that is so common among Pagans leads them to believe that they can cure themselves—and that if they "succumb" to a mental condition, they were just not eating the right diet, not giving adequate offerings to their god(s), or maybe not meditating or visualizing hard enough. Another reason is that in some cases Pagans believe that they deserve mental illness because by working with so-called negative influences such as dark gods and goddesses or the shadow side, they are actively inviting ailments such as depression or psychosis into their lives. Then there are those who adamantly refuse to even consider taking medication because they claim it will worsen health problems, lead to addiction, or diminish their mystical and/or creative abilities.

This last point of view is a conviction that I held for years and, unfortunately, was based on some real experiences. After being diagnosed with bipolar, I had a bad reaction to my main medication that threatened my physical health. In addition, the other meds that I had been prescribed after that incident were causing negative side effects, such as mental fogginess that alternated with panic attacks. I was also unconvinced that I even needed treatment, believing myself to be an artist and a freethinker who was clearly misunderstood by society (a classic bipolar rationalization). That, coupled with my medication ordeals, pushed me over the edge into complete denial

of my condition. I spent the next eleven years trying to manage my symptoms and my illness on my own unsuccessfully. I dropped out of school, had a difficult time maintaining a job, was plagued by numerous relationship problems, and used drugs and alcohol to self-medicate. After a long period of depression, I started to feel suicidal and relented in my decision to refuse treatment. I got psychiatric help and turned my life around, and aside from some regret over my "lost decade," I have never looked back.

Realistic Expectations

My story should not be seen as an endorsement of medication or other forms of therapy, because there is no one-size-fits-all solution. But I can say with certainty that if you think you need help, you should explore all possible avenues of medical care and intervention. Resisting treatment for a mental illness makes about as much sense as refusing to put a broken arm in a cast—not only will it never heal quite right, but the process will be slow and painful and you may permanently lose full use of the arm. The same is true for the mind. Mental health conditions are not given the same level of importance as physical ones because they are not readily apparent, so a mental illness can go untreated or even undetected for years. People may be drawn to Paganism because Pagans tend

Pagans tend to be highly individualistic people and are often cited for their sensitivity and introverted behavior. It's no wonder then that we attract those who feel uncomfortable in mainstream society, including people with a mental illness.

to be highly individualistic people and are often cited for their sensitivity and introverted behavior. It's no wonder then that we attract those who feel uncomfortable in mainstream society, including people with a mental illness, because we offer them a niche where they can hide out.

It is also important to remember that not everyone with a mental illness acts badly, and not everyone who acts badly has a mental illness. I'm sure you have met people in a Pagan context who are overly dramatic, self-serving, or inconsiderate of others, and/or are constantly seeking attention, causing conflict, or playing the victim. This kind of conduct may be exhibited by anyone, but the sad fact is that if a person has known mental health issues, people always look to place the blame on that first. And so sometimes those of us who act functional are accepted to be "sane," whereas those who are disruptive may be accused of having a mental illness. This is why covens and groups should address the undesirable behavior and not condemn the person or speculate whether or not they have a mental illness. First and foremost, that individual is a person—not a disability, not an illness, not a condition, and not a diagnosis.

Here's why a diagnosis, which can be used as a tool of self-understanding, can also be a curse that follows you everywhere: even when you don't reveal its existence, you know in the back of your mind that the diagnosis is still there and you can't help but wonder if others can "see" it and if they are judging you. Therefore, I think that full disclosure is a good thing: you can weed out those around you who might discriminate, and if you meet some compassionate and accepting Pagans, they can be supportive of your treatment and, as friends, can serve as an early warning system for potential mental health problems creeping up on you. It's also a great way to show others that those with mental health disorders aren't the violent and unpredictable monsters that the media portrays, but are just regular people like everyone else who have a few extra challenges to contend with.

Words of Caution and Parting Thoughts

I was taught the "skills and pills" philosophy of treatment, which is simply that medication and therapy go hand in hand, and that one is not much good without the other. Yet I hear all the time about people in therapy who refuse to cooperate or go off their meds despite their doctor's orders. Needless to say, no matter how supportive you are of anyone with a mental illness, it is still that person's choice whether or not they want to work at improving their mental health. You can't "save" anyone from themselves. You can, however, help people make good choices as long as they are receptive to them. On the subject of prescriptions, I have often heard the complaint that antidepressants can block the ability to sense the paranormal. However, isn't it better to feel well enough to participate more fully in other aspects of

spirituality? Also, it is very possible that the medications you are taking aren't right for you. I tried a whole bunch of them before I found ones that work for me, and while it was an arduous process, it was worth it to finally feel productive, happy, and whole.

Just as with spirituality, each person has to travel their own path to wellness. And there are some situations where a person is so lost on that path that you may have to consider ejecting them from your group or coven or avoid them entirely. I also caution against including individuals in practices that may "trigger" certain forms of mental illness. For example, you probably wouldn't want to serve alcohol in a circle that includes a person in Alcoholics Anonymous recovery or practice skyclad with someone diagnosed with a sex addiction.

Similarly, other situations or conditions may arise that intensify other forms of mental illness. Raising energy, energetic exchange, trance, communication with the spirit world, etc., can all trigger imbalances and even certain forms of psychosis. Most mental illnesses require therapy, medication, a lot of self-searching and introspection, and continued alertness to a possible relapse. With that being said, I don't think you will permanently aggravate someone's mental condition accidentally. Simply be aware, reserve judgment, show compassion, and treat the person equally—in essence, include them in your circle of "perfect love and perfect trust," and there's no reason anyone with a mental illness can't be just as spiritual as anyone else.

Autumn Damiana is an author, artist, crafter, and amateur photographer. She is a Solitary Eclectic Cottage Witch who has been following her Pagan path for almost two decades and is a regular contributor to Llewellyn's annuals. Along with writing and making art, Autumn is currently finishing up her degree in early childhood education. She lives with her husband and doggie familiar in the beautiful San Francisco Bay Area. Visit her online at autumndamiana.com.

Illustrator: Tim Foley

Advice for the Advisors: Tips for the Aspiring Psychic

Reverend J. Variable x/ø

So you've been working on your divination skills for quite a while now. You're pretty good with your tools: tarot, astrology, runes, or what have you. Friends are always hitting you up for advice, and when you're invited to a party, the host will invariably ask you to "bring your cards!"

Maybe it's time to start getting serious about this.

Psychic guidance is a booming market. There are usually at least two or three tarot booths at festivals and other eclectic events. You'll find ads for psychics in the back pages of newspapers and posted on community boards at neighborhood shops. On the Internet, thousands of independent readers compete with flashy professional websites boasting large teams of big-name advisors.

On one hand, all the public enthusiasm is kind of nice for us professional psychics. Non-believers just roll their eyes and move on, and we usually can ignore the extremists who want to set us on fire when the crops go bad. On the other hand, the saturated market makes for tough competition, and it's hard for potential clients to discern between the real deal and the charlatans who prey on desperate people.

How does a beginner break into this scene and start making a name for themselves?

I've been reading tarot cards and interpreting astrology charts for over twenty years. About five years ago, I started setting up my table as a small-time reader at local bars and events. I've also been on a team of psychic "experts" on one of those big flashy websites. Right now I operate mostly online, working from my own website and with another small group of friends on another site.

I've learned a lot about the mundane side of mysticism, so I've compiled some tips for my up-and-coming colleagues who wish to explore this as a career path. This isn't about reaching celebrity status or using clever tricks to dupe the gullible, though. The life of an honest psychic advisor is not terribly glamorous. We're basically glorified counselors who happen to use an unusual set of tools. It's hard work. I spend more time communing with my online ad settings and website codes than I do with my spirit guides (although one of my guides is a tech geek too, so that helps).

Despite the long hours and aggravation, when a client comes back to tell you how your insights improved (or even saved) their life, you'll remember why you got into this in the first place.

"Cross My Palm with Silver... Oh, Sure, I Take Plastic Too"

A big debate in magical circles is whether or not we should ask for money in return for spiritual services. There are good arguments on both sides. Some say it's unethical to demand material payment for using your god(s)-given spiritual talents. Others say it's equally unethical to demand that someone with any kind of talent donate their time and energy for free.

A big debate in magical circles is whether or not we should ask for money in return for spiritual services. Some say it's unethical to demand material payment for using your god(s)-given spiritual talents. Others say it's equally unethical to demand that someone with any kind of talent donate their time and energy for free.

You can probably guess which side I'm on. I double as a freelance designer, too, so I often find myself explaining to friends and strangers that I simply can't afford to work for free no matter how much I (or they) love what I do. Being able to feed my family doesn't corrupt my psychic intuition any more than it does my artistic skills. Even if I had a conventional full-time job to pay the bills, I sure wouldn't have enough juice left at the end of the day to do free psychic work for everyone who wants it (and when you give it away, believe me, people want it).

The decision of whether or not to charge money is up to you. I will occasionally do a free reading as a favor for a friend or as a special promotion. Don't feel guilty about asking for what you need in return for what you provide. Likewise, those who feel spiritually compelled to work for free are certainly welcome to do so. There's enough room in the field for all of us to find our own path.

Hanging Your Shingle

Once you're ready to get to work, you have to let customers know you're there. One of the best ways to attract attention is to perform in public. Bring your tools—and your business cards—to events, restaurants, and taverns. This is where a few free readings between friends can turn into profit! Make sure the crowd can see you reading for your companions. Curious onlookers become paying customers pretty quickly if you have a fast, cheap option for readings that you can do on the spot. Take advantage of the smartphone apps and tools (like credit card readers) that allow you to accept payment other than cash.

If you've got a website (and you should), small pay-per-click ads are worth the investment. My Google AdWords campaign is set to charge me no more than one dollar per day, and it brings around 200 to 300 visitors to my site every week.

Don't forget the power of social media, either. It's the digital equivalent of working a party. Start a business page for yourself on Facebook. Encourage your friends to spread the word, and join some of the professional discussion groups devoted to your psychic specialties. If you post a lot of interesting content and offer free short promotional readings every few days, you'll attract plenty of followers.

Do It Yourself

With all the material already out there to help us interpret cards and charts, it might be tempting to just cut and paste some of this pre-written text into your own written work. Don't! This is plagiarism, a violation of copyright laws, and a serious disservice to your clients.

Even if you've purchased interpretive software that includes a license to sell the reports it generates, it's still a bad idea to let the machine do it for you. For example, many of the big sites lead people to believe that they'll be working one on one with a real famous psychic, and charge several hundred dollars for the privilege. Imagine the client's disappointment (and wrath) when they realize that the reading that promised to change their lives is just some impersonal nonsense cobbled together by a computer program. I've seen it happen, and the damage control is not fun.

I do recommend using software to *create* astrology charts. There are also programs that will set up a tarot or rune reading by random selection, and if you can work with that, by all means, take advantage of the digital age. It's handy to prepare some of your own reusable material, too, so you don't have to type the same basic introductory information over and over again, but use these inserts sparingly. They should not make up the bulk of your readings. Your clients want a real connection with someone who will listen to them and offer thoughtful insights into their unique situation. Originality will set you apart and earn you a good reputation.

That Awful Disclaimer

Let's say it together: "For Entertainment Purposes Only." Doesn't that feel a little icky? Your insights have proven value! You help people understand their lives and solve their problems! It's not just "entertainment," it's counseling and wisdom of the highest order! It's...

It's a lawsuit waiting to happen is what it is. Yes, most of your clients will either sing your praises or simply disappear after one or two readings, leaving you to assume that they're satisfied. But there's always that one.

People are desperate to know what's going on with their job, their money, their marriage, their health, and other stressful concerns. They may come to you as a last resort, seeking clear-cut answers, because they just don't know what else to do (or they know very well what they should do and they want someone to give them permission not to do it). A good psychic provides useful information and constructive suggestions, but every reading has its fuzzy edges. No matter how great your track record may be, clients struggling with medical, legal, or financial issues must understand that your insights are not a replacement for professional help. If you intentionally allow someone to believe that everything will go their way if they just do what you say, you could be setting yourself up for legal trouble.

A good psychic provides useful information and constructive suggestions, but every reading has its fuzzy edges. No matter how great your track record may be, clients struggling with medical, legal, or financial issues must understand that your insights are not a replacement for professional help.

You can't control what people think, of course. A few clients will stubbornly cling to the idea that you're the ultimate authority and that once you've spoken, the responsibility of decision-making is off their shoulders. The icky disclaimer ensures that, legally, it's not on yours, either.

Presentation

A psychic cultivates (at least) two personas. You're a spiritual counselor, but you'll also find yourself "on stage" a lot. Learn to love both sides of this business and make that entertainment clause earn its keep!

When you're working a party or other public scene, most people will approach you because they're curious and looking for a thrill. However, readings can stir up some pretty intense emotions that aren't always appropriate for every environment. I try to set up my table in a quiet corner so clients have a little privacy, but sometimes this isn't possible. Don't blurt out someone's uncomfortable secrets in front of the whole room. Instead, use this as an opportunity to nail down future appointments.

A couple of well-placed hints from you will give them a little shiver when they realize that you couldn't possibly have just guessed that information. These are tantalizing hooks that will bring them back to you for a personal session where you can get off the stage and help them confront their deeper questions in an emotionally safe space.

On a related note, once a reading is finished, keep records. Hold on to the charts or take photos of the spread. Save the emails you exchange with your clients, and make notes during in-person sessions. Review this material before the client's next appointment so you can ease smoothly into the new reading. It makes you look good, and they'll appreciate not having to remind you of everything you've discussed already.

Questions, Questions

Thanks to ancient superstitions, Hollywood hyperbole, and our own marketing propaganda, there are a lot of misconceptions among the general public regarding what a psychic is actually able to do.

"Will he break up with her and come back to me?"

"What will my new boss do with our department?"

"On what date will my house sell and how much will I get for it?"

"What are next week's lotto numbers?"

"When will I die?"

Emotional pain and insecurity make people eager to pay good money to be told the whole story: who, what, when, where, and why. Some clients ask for such specific details that I wonder why they don't just hire a private investigator. Jealous lovers and betrayed friends want to know names, dates, locations, and detailed thought processes for all parties involved.

Destiny isn't assigned, it's created. And psychic intuition is not literally "mind reading." We psychics have a gift that enables us to gauge the prevailing energy currents, sense probabilities, dig into another's psyche, and determine whether a course of action is likely to bring a positive or negative result. Free will ensures that the energy is always changing, though. No psychic I've ever met can correctly predict exactly what will happen in a situation that depends on individual choices. (If you can do that consistently and on command, I'd very much like to meet you! Also, you could have a much more profitable career than that of a psychic advisor. Go into advertising or play the stock market. You'll make a mint.)

When your client asks, "Will this happen?" explain why it would be more helpful to ask, "What can I do to improve my chances for success?" Try to get a feel for the underlying essence of the situation, and once the initial questions have been addressed, turn their attention to the deeper complexities (or simplicities) that brought them to this point in the first place.

A simple question can easily turn into a series of involved readings. That's good for your wallet, but it brings us to another gray area. Of course you want repeat business, but like any professional advisor, your job is to help people identify and solve their problems, rather than allowing them to become dependent on your guidance for every little thing. Know when to stop. At some point, you'll have done everything you can for them, and more readings won't help—they have to take action to meet the challenges in their lives and create the changes they want to see.

And those folks who want the winning lotto numbers? I'm not sure why they think anyone with that kind of information would be working as a psychic. If you can do that trick, I'll gladly pay you a couple hundred bucks for a reading…after my mega-million jackpot check clears.

Reverend J. Variable x/ø *is a cyber sorcerer, an urban druid, a chaos mage, an artist, and a web designer (not necessarily in that order). It lives in Portland, Oregon, with one yellow snake, two fuzzy tarantulas, a very nervous parakeet, and a fine Husband-Thing who enthusiastically encourages the pursuit of any crazy idea as long as the bills get paid. Variable can be found online hawking metaphysical wares and services at http://reverend-variable.com.*

Illustrator: Bri Hermanson

The Dark Aspects of Bright-Siding

Charlie Rainbow Wolf

There's been a lot of hype over the last few years about the law of attraction. Rhonda Byrne wrote about it in her 2006 book *The Secret*, which was also turned into a blockbuster movie. Oprah raved about it. People swore it changed their lives. But was it really such a big secret? Or was it all just hype?

The Secret is the latest version of the law of attraction, but the law of attraction has been doing the rounds for over a hundred years, starting with William W. Atkinson. In his book *Thought Vibration; or, The Law of Attraction in the Thought World*, first published in 1906, he talks

about thought being a manifestation of energy—the same topic covered in *The Secret*. From these publications, we might be led to think that all we have to do is want something badly enough in order to get it. In reality, this rarely happens. Synchronicity does occur, but it's rarely just because of thinking positive thoughts. It takes more than that to create the life we want to live. In fact, just thinking positive thoughts and wishing for good things could actually be detrimental to the desired outcome.

Let's start by looking at the word *want*. It can be defined as desire, but it can also be defined as to be without, to be deficient, or to fall short. Every time we say we want something, not only are we expressing that we desire it but we're also confirming that it is not in our lives, that we're left *wanting*. If we say we want something, we're sending a message out into the cosmos that we're deficient in this desire. If the law of attraction teaches that like energy attracts like energy, then by confirming we're lacking in what we want, we're attracting the lack of it into our lives. It starts to get complicated, doesn't it?

This is where so many people seem to slip up. It's easier to bright-side at this point. Bright-siding is always looking on the bright side of things but not really doing anything constructive. It's the naive belief that if someone is just optimistic enough or if something is wanted badly enough, then it will happen and everything will be okay. I've even seen bright-siders criticize those who are looking at things in a realistic manner in order to find a practical solution! That's when the whole positive-thinking trap starts to collapse. Optimism is one thing, but optimism without a call to action for a solution is just delusional.

This doesn't mean that there is no merit to the law of attraction. It has some validity. It's just not as simple as desiring something badly enough to wish it into existence. It would be delightful if all we had to do to manifest our desires was ask for it and then wait for it to happen. In fact, some people even bring quantum physics into it. It's easy to buy into this, because quantum physics consists of the seen and the unseen. Science has already proven that everything in the cosmos is just energy vibrating at one frequency or another. It might be plausible to think that if we align

This doesn't mean that there is no merit to the law of attraction. It has some validity. It's just not as simple as desiring something badly enough to wish it into existence.

our energy with the energy of our desires, then we become one. It doesn't work quite like that, though.

In a 1944 speech, German physicist Max Planck said: "All matter originates and exists only by virtue of a force... We must assume behind this force the existence of a conscious and intelligent Mind. This Mind is the matrix of all matter."

What Planck is telling us is that we control that matter with our thoughts. This is where the bright-siders and those who work with the law of attraction can get deluded into believing that all they have to do is think of something and it will happen. It takes a bit more than thought to bring things into being, and this is where a lot of the disappointment and disillusionment over the law of attraction starts to arise. If we want to lose weight, and we think about losing weight, and we believe that the law of attraction will cause us to lose weight but we sit on the sofa eating potato chips all day, what's going to happen?

It's very clear why so many folks were taken in by the claims that this belief system works. For one, all that seems to be needed is to think about what is desired—no work involved, right? Wrong. If we know what we want, it's great to visualize it and be open to receiving it, but we also have to make it a priority in order for it to become a reality. Wanting something leaves us wanting. Let's face it: if all we had to do was ask for and believe in a good job or a happy marriage, then there'd be no unemployment and no divorce. Also, consider this: what if more than one person wanted the same job, or even the same spouse? What then? For whom does the law of attraction work in that situation? How is the successful person chosen?

I know it might sound like I'm really bashing all of this stuff, but I'm not. I'm approaching it in a realistic way—a way in which common sense, reasoning, positive thinking, and action can be used to create what is desired. It's got little to do with energy and more to do with focus. It's more a question of priorities than quantum physics. The problem is that hucksters are always going to try to sell to the gullible, and if they can get the gullible to believe that all that is necessary for success is to think good things and life will be good, then they've got a captive audience, for it is human nature to want the easy way out. That's where the trouble begins. In order for this to work, we have to stay connected to the process, not make a wish and wait for it to come true.

There is a way that the power of positive thinking can help us achieve our goals. Psychologists call it the *confirmation bias*. This means that we all have a tendency to seek out information that supports what we want to believe. We choose where we want to place our focus. It is human nature to pay more attention to what we want to believe, or what we have been conditioned to believe, than to think outside the box. Things that challenge us make us uncomfortable—but often they're just what we need in order to achieve our goals.

It's very easy to use the confirmation bias to talk ourselves into or out of something. For example, if you're on the fence about a relationship and you hear something bad about that person, it would be easy to look back and highlight other instances from the past that validate what you've heard, making it easier for you to decide to break off the relationship. If you're besotted with the person and you hear something bad about them, then you're more likely to look back and find things that contradict what you've heard, making it easier for you to decide to work on the relationship.

Bright-siders will tell you that in order to fix that relationship, all you have to do is think positive thoughts about it and it will be mended. Because of the confirmation bias, you'll focus on the positive side of things and you'll trust that everything is going to be okay. Likewise, if you focus on the negative aspects, you'll start to worry that things are falling apart—and then the bright-siders will tell you it's because you were thinking negative thoughts that the relationship deteriorated. The truth is that it takes more than thinking to make or break a situation.

The danger of bright-siding is that people can become unrealistically positive about things, and then the confirmation bias leads them to believe that they're right. While this can help those who have spent their lives in a negative headspace to cultivate a more optimistic outlook on things, to feel better about themselves, and to find reasons to enjoy their lives, it's not a panacea for everything or everyone.

If someone really buys into bright-siding, thinking that all they have to do is to believe in themselves and think positive thoughts to achieve their goals, then they can easily set themselves up for failure. Without research or even common sense (which often flies out the window when we want something badly enough), speculative investments could result in financial loss, toxic relationships might be cultivated, or health matters could be ignored. Why would a logical person behave in this manner? Because they've bought into the concept of bright-siding so vehemently that they're not listening to reason. Optimism has its place, but not when it replaces rationality.

Another downfall of bright-siding is that it can actually create the opposite mental process. It often happens that the very minute someone tells us not to think of something, that's immediately where our brain goes. Maybe we're trying to quit smoking and we suddenly notice how we are more acutely aware of people smoking around us, of the discarded cigarette butts on the ground, or of just how many shops sell cigarettes and smoking sundries. Perhaps we're trying to lose weight and we see just how many fast-food restaurants are in our neighborhood, or just how many people are snacking around us, or how many times we open the fridge out of habit. Thinking about the things we don't want to do can give them greater focus and more importance in our lives. Rather than concentrating on wishing for a change to take place, wishing for it to be true, it's better to focus on alternative activities, to retrain our brains to think of things other than what we're trying to avoid.

This isn't to say that we shouldn't remain optimistic in our determination, because we absolutely should. Let's revisit the weight-loss scenario. It's better to reinforce the desire to lose weight by going to the gym instead of the donut shop. That way we're doing something positive and making beneficial changes in our lives. The detrimental behavior would be to go to the donut shop and eat whatever we wish but believe we're still losing weight. There's a difference!

Bright-siding can lead us to failure. If we believe that all we have to do to get a job or pass a test or lose weight is to remain positive, then we are likely to put forth less effort and then be disappointed when someone who was equally confident but tried a bit harder succeeded where we did not.

Other people can be detrimental to our progress and may be part of our bright-siding downfall, too. They often mean well, but if they too are buying into the law of attraction and believing that all they have to do is desire something and it will manifest, then they could be encouraging us to do likewise. They may be offering platitudes and other ways of helping us stay in a positive mindset but doing very little to help us make real headway toward our ultimate goal. Yes, we feel better in their company, but are we actually accomplishing anything?

Bright-siding can alienate us from people who genuinely want to help. Let's go back to the donut shop example. If a person is eating whatever is desired because the law of attraction says that as long as belief in weight loss is held then weight loss will happen, then that person is likely to get very angry at a colleague who points out that perhaps a different way of eating might be more appropriate and effective than just wishing to lose weight. It's hard to reason with people who are fanatical about anything they vehemently believe in, and that can lead to relationships deteriorating when others aren't so enthusiastic about the power of positive thinking being the only tool needed.

Our chances of success can become limited by bright-siding, too. When we wait for something to happen instead of working toward it, the likelihood of realizing the goal dissipates rather than increases. Would an athlete dream of winning an Olympic gold medal without putting in the hours of training and having the determination to succeed? Still, some folks seem to think that believing in the law of attraction is all they need to do to win. This is a catalyst for failure rather than an effective strategy for success.

Emotions can also get in the way. Yes, we can think good thoughts all day long, but if something happens to us that puts our stomach in knots and our emotions into a tailspin, then those emotions are going to overpower our thought process, no matter how hard we try to prevent this from happening. Those feelings are there for a reason, and to try to bright-side them into unimportance could be extremely detrimental.

No matter how positive we think, challenges are going to arise. We're going to be disappointed. Then we have two options. We can

sit on the sofa and wonder why the law of attraction let us down again and get totally despondent about it, or we can look that disappointment in the eye and determine why we feel that way, what our emotions are trying to tell us, and how best to handle the situation to bring about a positive outcome. When negative feelings arise as a result of a disappointment, we need to remember to treat ourselves with compassion and then see how we can make the best of things. There's a difference between bright-siding and actively working toward a positive outcome.

When we begin to use positive thinking to help us on our journey, many of us get off on the wrong foot. We say things like "I don't want to be fat" or "I don't want to be in debt" or "I don't want to be lonely." Stating goals in negative phrasing rather than as something positive can actually hinder rather than help our progress, so we always want to phrase our goals in positive ways. This is called using *empowered language*. It assists in priming our brain to better engage us in reaching our goals. In the previous examples, the mind is focusing on "fat," "debt," and "lonely," yet those are the opposite of what is desired! It is better to think in the positive so that the brain latches onto the goal rather than the failure. In this case, the more appropriate phrasings would be "I am going to be slender," "I am going to be financially independent," and "I am going to be content." We could even argue that it might be better to replace the phrase "am going to be" with the word "am," so that we're not constantly projecting our goal into the future but are living it in the now.

Becoming a better person in order to have what we desire isn't as easy as believing it's going to happen, nor should it be. In his 2008 book *The Last Lecture*, Randy Pausch says: "The brick walls are there for a reason. The brick walls are not there to keep us out; the brick walls are there to give us a chance to show how badly we want something. The brick walls are there to stop the people who don't want it badly enough. They are there to stop the *other* people!"

We grow not just by thinking good thoughts but by thinking those thoughts and then following them up with action and determination. Yes, we will be challenged. Yes, we will falter, we will err, and we will miscalculate. An optimistic approach doesn't make it impossible to fail; it gives us the tenacity to get up and try again. It's harder work, but it's also going to bring results rather than the bewilderment that we didn't get what we wished for simply by believing it would come effortlessly to us. Visualizing what we want is only the first step of the journey. We have to be active in the process if we want to achieve the goal.

This is where many of us fall down. We have this goal in our mind, we have the positive affirmation, we're taking steps to achieve the goal, and we scare ourselves witless. Why? Because most people are far more afraid of succeeding than of failing. We're taught that if we don't believe in ourselves, then why should anyone else believe in us? Most of us latch onto our failures and beat ourselves up over them, rather than focusing on our successes and celebrating them. Anyone who has worked in retail will understand this. There may have been dozens of great customers that day, but it is the encounter with the one nasty one that the brain replays over and over again, right?

So what can be done? Well, first we can acknowledge that the law of attraction works in order to help us get into the right mindset for success, but we have to act on those thoughts if we want to make them manifest.

So what can be done? Well, first we can acknowledge that the law of attraction works in order to help us get into the right mindset for success, but we have to act on those thoughts if we want to make them manifest. If we use the law of attraction for motivation, if we use it as a catalyst for determination and claim that goal as ours, then it can help us see the confirmation bias that will help us achieve our intention. Second, remember that Max Planck taught us that we can control matter with our thoughts. This doesn't mean that we only have to think something and it will happen. However, when we envision our goals in a positive way, we can start to create openings. Then, using the confirmation bias, we see those openings, and if we seize the opportunities, then we can achieve our objectives.

Finally, let's think about this: If the law of attraction states that all we have to do is focus on and wish for what we want and it will happen, then that's teaching us to always be wanting something. Those affirmations that we think are leading us to success may actually be impeding it! At the end of the day, happiness is often found not in getting what we want but in wanting what we have.

Sources

Atkinson, William W. *Thought Vibration; or, The Law of Attraction in the Thought World*. Reprint, CreateSpace Independent Publishing Platform, 2008.

Byrne, Rhonda. *The Secret*. Hillsboro, OR: Atria Books/Beyond Words, 2006.

Byrne, Rhonda, and Paul Harrington, producers. *The Secret*. DVD. TS Production LLC, 2006.

Nickerson, Raymond S. "Confirmation Bias: A Ubiquitous Phenomenon in Many Guises." *Review of General Psychology* Vol. 2, No. 2 (1998): 175–220. Educational Publishing Foundation. http://landman-psychology.com /ConfirmationBias.pdf.

Pausch, Randy. *The Last Lecture*. New York: Hyperion, 2008.

Charlie Rainbow Wolf *is happiest when she's creating something, especially if it can be made from items that others have cast aside. Pottery, writing, knitting, astrology, and tarot are her deepest interests, but she happily confesses that she's easily distracted because life offers so many wonderful things to explore. She is an advocate of organic gardening and cooking and lives in the Midwest with her husband and special-needs Great Danes. Visit her at www.charlierainbow.com.*

Illustrator: Neil Brigham

Are Pagans Required to Be Environmentalists?

Lupa

When I first discovered Paganism in the 1990s, it was common for Pagans to refer to themselves as practitioners of "earth-based religions." A lot of this had to do with the increasing popularity of Wicca at the time, not just in the Pagan community but in general. Non-Pagans often reacted negatively to the rise of Witchcraft in their communities, partly due to lurid rumors of devil worship and evil deeds. So, in self-defense, many Wiccans and other Pagans began to emphasize their spiritual connections to nature. This helped to open more constructive dialogues with non-Pagans, but it also cemented the idea in many people's minds that Paganism equals nature worship.

They're not entirely wrong. Lots of Pagans follow very nature-centered paths, myself included. However, there are Pagans whose paths are centered on the worship of the gods or spirits, or the reconstruction of pre-Christian religions. These Pagans may not consider their spirituality to be anything more than peripherally related to nature at best.

This doesn't mean Pagans can't be environmentalists even if they aren't earth-based in their beliefs. There's no holy writ that forces us to be more eco-conscious, though. In fact, we're just as likely as the rest of the population to throw cigarette butts on the ground, burn fossil fuels, and throw out some of the food we buy. Our altars are full of tools and decorations made from petroleum-based plastic and metals mined with polluting byproducts, manufactured

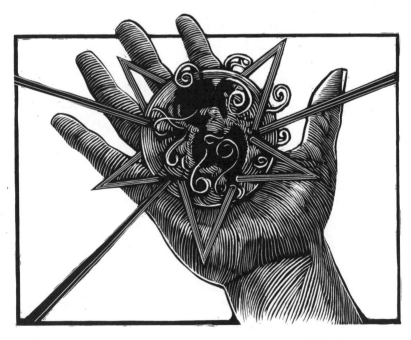

in filthy factories by abused workers, and sent overseas on massive ships leaking oil into the ocean.

Despite this, we are still not *required* to be environmentalists. Humans have wreaked great devastation on the planet, yet we are creatures of free will: there is no universal law that stops us from consuming all of the resources left to us. If we wanted to, we could be a species of Neros fiddling while the whole Earth burned.

Yet plenty of us want to avoid that desperate, final fate. So we try to walk lightly on the land and encourage others to do the same, through education and example. Pagans don't have to be environmentalists, but for those who choose that path, please consider the following spiritual-environmental connections to help guide you on your way.

Nature-Based Paganism

You'd think that all proclaimed nature-based Pagans would be environmentalists, wouldn't you? Yet "nature-based" has a lot of different interpretations. On one end of the spectrum we have people for whom environmentalism is a religion in and of itself, clothed in mythos and meaning but rooted firmly in the physical world. Every act and every breath is in service to the planet and its denizens, and these Pagans make every choice they can with that devotion in mind. They may go so far as to attack other Pagans for being "not committed enough," though I don't recommend that as an effective way to win over hearts and minds.

At the other end of the spectrum are Pagans who give lip service to the earth. They'll speak of the sacredness of the seasons and animals and nature's beauty in ritual but will then turn around and serve the ritual feast on disposable, non-biodegradable styrofoam plates. There's a fundamental disconnect between what they say is sacred and how that translates into their behaviors.

Most of us nature-based Pagans fall somewhere in the middle. Perfection is a pretty impossible standard to uphold, so we make mistakes even though we know better. But unlike some religions that guilt-trip you for every single screw-up you make, Paganism allows you to be human and therefore imperfect.

That means that even if you can't be what you see as a "perfect" environmentalist, you're still making a difference whenever you try your best under the circumstances. You might not have as much money or time or energy to give, but most Pagans don't get to practice their religion as consistently as they'd like. In the end, all environmentalism—or, if you prefer, conservationism—is in service to the earth. All that's needed for a nature-based Pagan to make that service spiritual is to add your intent to your actions and to see those actions as sacred. Beyond that, it's up to you as to how closely the two are intertwined.

Deity/Spirit-Based Paganism

Let me preface this section by saying there are a *lot* of deities and spirits out there, far more than I can discuss in this one little article. Some of them are very blatantly nature-based—gods of storms, spirits of rivers, totems, fey beings, and so forth. Others may seem further removed, such as techno-spirits in computers and cars.

In the end, all of them can be traced back to nature in one way or another. Zeus is easily embodied in the wild storms that pass overhead. Computer hardware is made of silicon, copper, petroleum, and other natural materials, though it is reformed by human processes. We humans are primate mammals ourselves, and our actions are extensions of our complex animal nature and needs. Aphrodite may have floated in on a seashell, but the love she brings forth is based in a chemical process in the brains and bodies of many animals.

All of the houses of the spirits and gods, everything they embody and represent—ultimately it all comes from nature. We have only fooled ourselves into thinking we're separate from the rest of nature. By reforming that connection to the natural world, we also strengthen our bond with the spirits and deities that are as much a part of it as we are.

One of the best ways to honor these beings is to honor the nature that they're connected to. You might clean trash out of a river as an offering to the spirits who live there, or you could recycle an old computer rather than throwing it out as a sacred act to the techno-spirits in it as well as the spirits of the minerals, metals, and other components. If a particular animal is sacred to a deity you worship, do something to help the species, like donating toward its conservation or not buying products that threaten its habitat.

Culture-Based Paganism

Culture-based Paganism is really a whole selection of Pagan traditions, each with its own unique community and practices and traditions. Some of these paths are deeply rooted in the ways of a particular culture, while others are more eclectic in their sourcing. What's important to keep in mind here is each culture's attitude toward the environment, as well as your own personal feelings on the matter. After all, cultures are made of individuals, not hive-minds.

Some of these communities have deep-seated connections with the natural world. There may already be long-practiced ways to honor the earth and treat it well. Some of these may have been interrupted or even lost due to oppression by other cultures, illnesses that devastated entire populations, or loss of oral traditions. That makes it even more crucial to protect the traditions that are still there.

Other cultures may have lost their connection with the natural world entirely, or at least think they have. Here it's important to create new eco-friendly traditions and practices, as it is these cultures that most frequently lead the way in environmental devastation. Spirituality brings people together in incredibly strong ways, and through rites and shared social mores, positive changes can be brought about.

A culture is, in part, an expression of the relationship between the people and the land. Spirituality is one of the most vulnerable and powerful manifestations of this bond. By practicing environmentally friendly ways and creating new ones where needed, you are honoring both the culture you are a part of and its spiritual path.

Putting the Sacred into Action

So what can we do to counteract the daily assault on the earth, even if we're limited in finances or lacking in time or energy?

A lot of this comes down to everyday choices. What we eat, where we live, how we get from place to place—all of this affects our relationship with nature. Some of the easiest environmental actions start at home. If these actions are daily devotionals, then more intensive volunteer efforts are sacred rituals. Many areas have environmental groups of some sort to which we can donate our time, doing everything from litter pickup to invasive species removal to pollution monitoring. In the absence of such organizations, just going out and collecting litter can make a huge difference. Try going out on the sabbats or esbats, or on other sacred days in your path.

But what of offerings? Leaving a sprinkling of small crystals or a splash of water at a ritual site may be romantic, but in the long run it is ineffective on a practical level, as it makes no positive, physical change to the place. If you want to make a bigger impact and you're able to spare the funds, consider making a donation to an environmental group that helps protect local waterways or landscapes. Or make a gift to those who fight air pollution, climate change, and other widespread problems.

Many of the worst environmental ills are perpetrated by large entities such as governments and corporations. By sending letters to your elected officials or other people in power, and by voicing your concerns to companies (especially those trying to sell you something), you can let them know you are paying attention to their actions and you want them to make certain choices. It may feel intimidating trying to be one little voice, but if a lot of us stand up and speak, we're more likely to make a difference. Remember, you are one little voice, but there are a lot of "one little voices" refusing to be silent.

Finally, if you aren't indigenous to the place where you live, look into how the indigenous cultures relate to the land. Those are traditions and practices that have been developed over centuries, and while not every single one may be the best for the land, they often are more eco-friendly than newer alternatives. Just be respectful when inquiring about sensitive cultural traditions; don't barge in like the Great Environmentalist out to save the land. Instead, listen carefully and with humility when someone chooses to share their practices with you.

There are plenty of other ways to be a Pagan environmentalist. These are just a few suggestions. With time, you'll find routines and actions that work best for your lifestyle and resources, and learn how to adapt when your situation changes.

Recommended Resources

A Pagan Community Statement on the Environment, http://ecoPagan.com

Cultural Survival, www.culturalsurvival.org

National Audubon Society, www.audubon.org

Natural Resources Defense Council, www.nrdc.org

Peace Corps, "Environment," www.peacecorps.gov/volunteer/learn
   /whatvol/env

Rewild.com, http://rewild.com

Richard Louv, http://richardlouv.com

Volunteer Match, www.volunteermatch.org

Waterkeeper Alliance, http://waterkeeper.org

Lupa *is an author, artist, amateur naturalist, and wannabe polymath in Portland, Oregon. She is the author of several books on nature Pagan practices, including* Nature Spirituality From the Ground Up: Connect with Totems in Your Ecosystem *(Llewellyn, 2016), and is the creator of the* Tarot of Bones. *Her primary website is www.thegreenwolf.com.*

Illustrator: Rik Olson

The Dark Goddess as Initiator: Reading into Fairy Tale and Myth

Jane Meredith

In myths and fairy stories, the Dark Goddess and her counterparts—the wicked witch, the evil stepmother, Baba Yaga, or the thirteenth fairy—are terrifying. The Dark Goddess deals in death and fear, in curses and murderous intent. Often her actions and motivations come from a place of illogic; she is not someone who can be outwitted or outmaneuvered. And the focus of her attention is usually a young woman, even a girl, who is immature and has few resources or skills and little support— someone who has drawn her attention, or has crossed her path unwisely, or

needs something from her. On the face of it, you'd assume that the young girl has no chance, not even enough to create a story... but that's not what happens.

Psyche meeting up with Persephone, Inanna meeting up with Ereshkigal, Gretel with the Witch, Gerda with the Snow Queen, Vasalisa with Baba Yaga, Snow White with the Queen, Sleeping Beauty with the thirteenth fairy... they all triumph. They don't get eaten or destroyed. They do sometimes die, or go through a state very close to death, but then, with some twist in the story, they return to life. How could that be? Even within the realms of illogic and story-making, these dark-goddess figures are immeasurably more powerful than the girl they set out to destroy—unless something else is happening and that's not their motivation at all.

So there's a story underneath the story, and we have been misreading it all this time. A young girl and an older, much more powerful feminine force cross paths, and amid threats of death and destruction the young girl emerges wiser, more mature, empowered, and powerful. As Inanna famously repeats on her way down into the Underworld: *What is this?*

Our fear of this other—the witch, the Dark Goddess—is so strong that it carries us away, and, like a conjuring trick, while our attention is distracted, the important things are happening elsewhere. We rarely view these stories from the perspective of the older, more powerful female figure. Our eyes are usually on the young and innocent one—that is, a representation of ourselves when we meet Death or a powerful goddess, or inexplicable destruction. We know nothing. We are stuck in a mortal body that is under dire threat. And listening to the story, we assume that viewpoint (of the one who knows nothing) is accurate. But clearly, something is missing from that viewpoint—or else those characters wouldn't make it through the confrontation.

Let's look more closely at what actually happens in these stories. There's a girl or a young woman. Sometimes she sets out on a quest. Sometimes it's just due to the circumstances of her birth, but in one way or another she comes to the attention of an older, very powerful and usually magical feminine force. This version of the Dark Goddess either presents the girl with a challenge or creates a situation in which she will not be able to succeed, because usually she brings to it no magical powers, little knowledge or wisdom, and few skills or resources. Yet she survives, often due to simply having a good heart. Then the really fascinating part happens: she gains power, a level of power that either sets her free from the challenge or places her on an equal level with her challenger. Could this long list of wicked queens, evil witches, and Dark Goddesses be so collectively unlucky or miscalculate so as to fail every time?

Surely not. What we might take to be a simple moral tale of the triumph of good over evil is more complex, for usually the older, darker feminine is not destroyed. When we look even more closely, we see that in many of these stories the young girl now has potentially sinister powers of her own; to a certain degree, she has become her opponent. These are stories of youth maturing, of girls turning into women, of initiation into the  feminine by the feminine. A young girl becomes a woman by confronting darkness and power—you could say, her own darkness and power—and integrating them into herself. In this way, she wins her heart's desire. But she is no longer innocent. In accepting the challenge, in succeeding, she has become a version of what she battled against. She has been initiated. She is transformed.

. . . .

Stepping through the Snow White story night by night at a European Reclaiming WitchCamp, I became aware of this dynamic. As we unfolded the story gradually, it became clear to me that the Queen (Snow White's stepmother or, in older versions, mother) was providing some kind of initiation for Snow White—a severe one, but traditional in its symbolism—a death-and-rebirth experience. Snow White undergoes three near-death experiences, or four if you include her encounter with the hunter who is ordered by the Queen to kill her. This first encounter with near-death can be seen as the call to initiation, or the warning that the process has begun; it is the only one of her encounters with death where Snow White is not directly confronting the Queen.

The next three times Snow White encounters these death threats, her wits and choices count, to a certain extent. However, in the end, she succumbs to the tricks of the Queen, or to the demands of initiation. She bites into the apple—and what a metaphor that is for initiation—and falls into a death-like sleep. The fairy tale ending of a marriage with a prince can be read as just that, or as a Jungian development of the animus and integration of the self, or as an initiatory transition into queendom; for at the end of the story, Snow White has achieved a parallel state with her persecutor, the Queen. The transition in this story is from a helpless child at the mercy of others, to an adult woman with the friendship and loyalty of the dwarves (almost her own court), to queenship.

This completely changed the story for me and began to remind me of other tales where a powerful feminine character—portrayed as negative or even evil—actually provides the catalyst for the younger female character to find freedom, love, and power through rising to the challenge presented to her; in short, to be offered and to accept the initiation into womanhood. This appears to always involve meeting the powerful deathly feminine force on its own terms, changing or rewriting the terms dictated, and—essentially—integrating some of the power that was initially used against her into her own character and actions.

In the fairy tale of the Snow Queen, young Gerda quests through the seasons of the year in order to find her playmate Kay, whom the Snow Queen has stolen away. By the time Gerda rescues him, melting the splinters of ice that are lodged in his eye and heart with her tears of love, the two have matured from children to become lovers. In this story, Gerda is quite specifically told that she cannot be given any gifts to help vanquish the Snow Queen, that what she has herself (or who she is) must be enough. She risks death at several stages in her journey and in the Snow Queen's palace. Kay himself had not asked to be rescued—in fact, the opposite—and nearly everyone Gerda meets is determined to delay her indefinitely or dissuade her from continuing her quest. But once again, the Queen has provided an initiation for Gerda that has seen her mature from a girl into a woman.

There are other fairy tales where this role is played by a witch; Hansel and Gretel is one. These stories still have the theme of the young girl's fascination with the older, powerful feminine (evidenced as the compelling magic of the gingerbread cottage) and the necessity for the heroine to accept the witch's terms, then thwart her, turn the story around, and take that power to free herself. Gretel escapes the witch by tricking her and pushing her into the oven. She saves Hansel and herself and returns home, where her father has gotten rid of the stepmother who forced the children out into the forest.

This repeated theme, of a powerless girl undergoing an apparently impossible challenge and succeeding—and most especially as a transition into adulthood—looks to me like a meeting with the Dark Goddess. Add to that the fact that these queens carry all the powers of the Dark Goddess—life and death (for they are often in the position of mothers, and if not mothers, they are powerful magic practitioners)—as well as a lot of the characteristics that are projected, in our world, onto the dark feminine, or sometimes even just the powerful feminine. It seems to me that these queens are just one step removed

from the Dark Goddess and are playing out her role of powerful initiator of the feminine.

After the Sumerian Inanna, Queen of Heaven and Earth, has descended to the Underworld and been slain there by her sister, Ereshkigal, Queen of the Underworld, she rises again, reborn and with the powers of life and death integrated within her. This is made apparent both by the retinue of demons that she brings with her from the Underworld and by the fact that she now has the power to send others—first her consort and then his sister—to take her place in the Underworld. In other words, she holds the same powers of life and death as her sister.

In Greek mythology, when Psyche finally submits to undergoing Aphrodite's impossible tasks to win back her lover, Eros, she is eventually changed by the gods into an immortal, as well as being reunited with her love. But earlier in the tale, when Psyche is avoiding Aphrodite and asking for help from other gods and goddesses, it is made clear to her that the only hope she has is to directly approach the terrifying, all-powerful Aphrodite, who wishes her dead. Aphrodite sends Psyche to Persephone. Once you have come to the attention of the Dark Goddess, there is no other way through than by submitting to the tasks she sets before you, by undergoing her initiation, whatever that may be.

Persephone—who becomes Queen of the Underworld—is witnessed in her original descent (and possibly kidnapping, depending on which version of the story you follow) by Hecate, a much older dark queen, crone, or Dark Goddess. Persephone's challenge involves the direct integration of aspects of the Underworld, in the form of

Once you have come to the attention of the Dark Goddess, there is no other way through than by submitting to the tasks she sets before you, by undergoing her initiation, whatever that may be.

the pomegranate seeds, which may represent simply the food of the Underworld, the powers of rebirth, or her pregnancy by Hades. Once that has occurred, she can move between the upper and lower realms, although she is no longer a child or defined only by being her mother's daughter. She has taken on the challenge of the Dark Goddess and become Goddess of the Dark Realm, a maiden initiated into queen. Often it is asked why Hecate took no action at Persephone's descent to save her. I think that here is the answer. She was witnessing, or possibly even facilitating, an initiation.

Somehow these queens, with their dark and terrible powers, are creating initiations for girls into maturity and power. These tales, with their split feminine forces (one young, powerless, and "light" or good, and the other older, powerful, and dark or even evil), can be read as a reintegration of the two sides of the feminine. Beyond the faces of the bright goddess and the Dark Goddess is the face of the one goddess. Beyond the helpless young Snow White and her wicked stepmother is the mature Snow White, free, happy, and a queen in her own right. Beyond each of the polarities of these tales—the young girl facing a life-threatening challenge and the queen who seems to threaten her—is the end of these tales: the main character assuming an adult position in the world and an integration of power and the polarities within her.

. . . .

What good is it to know this? First, we have to understand what the dark feminine forces are in our own lives. I can easily name menarche, childbirth, and menopause as the traditional blood-related life-and-death moments. But perhaps our knowledge of the dark feminine comes from our relationship to our mother, or simply from being a woman or having a woman's body. In our society, such things are not ritually integrated and acknowledged as powerful initiators.

In this world of economic imperatives, institutional power, and disconnection from the sacred, the dark feminine is just as likely to manifest in ways such as depression, addiction, physical illness, mental or emotional instability, or being a victim of violence, abuse, or circumstance. There are also periods of vulnerability, grief, and trauma that each of us go through in our lives, plummeting us into realms where we are unrecognizable to ourselves and forced to confront our demons, our despair, and our disconnection from the life we have so carefully constructed.

To apply this learning, we have to say that these huge and frightening forces can be, in fact, initiations. They can be the gateway into power. They can be the raw material for our transition into maturity, the integration of the powerful and mature feminine—in other words, the initiation of the Dark Goddess.

As for how to transition through the initiation by the dark feminine, the stories are very clear on this. Look at Gerda, look at Inanna, look at Psyche or Snow White: not one of these characters will succeed if she does not accept the challenge, a challenge that usually appears to be impossible. Not one of them has a chance of success unless she follows her heart, what she knows to be right, although usually there is little or no confirmation of this in the world around her.

The Dark Goddess, or the wicked queen of the fairy tales, is seen as evil only by our eyes that have been taught to condemn the dark feminine—most particularly, the *power* of the dark feminine. It is

hardly surprising that within a patriarchy, these young (uninitiated) female characters are inevitably drawn to their powerful, older counterparts. This is perhaps even why we require this (often fairly rough) initiation/intervention of the "dark forces." We are not supported to achieve maturity and power; our culture conspires to keep us youthful, innocent, and powerless.

This wicked queen of many fairy tales, as the Dark Goddess in myths, forces her counterpart into a confrontation that she cannot escape. Although the young girl appears to lose everything, by the end she has gained her heart's desire, or—put another way—her wholeness and maturity.

It seems that there is no choice but to accept the challenge demanded of you by the dark queen and to follow your heart every step of the way. We can treat the Dark Goddess (or even her presentation in our lives as depression, crisis, or grief) as other and frightening. Or we can follow the storyline and recognize her as the force of the feminine that we are disconnected from and must, at any cost, meet and integrate as our own.

Jane Meredith *is an Australian author and ritualist. Her latest book, co-authored with Gede Parma, is* Magic of the Iron Pentacle: Reclaiming Sex, Pride, Self, Power & Passion. *Her previous books include* Circle of Eight: Creating Magic for Your Place on Earth *and* Journey to the Dark Goddess. *Jane is passionate about mythology, magic, dark chocolate, rivers, and trees. She teaches in-person and distance courses and also teaches in the Reclaiming Tradition. Her website is www.janemeredith.com.*

Illustrator: Jennifer Hewitson

Witchy Living

DAY-BY-DAY WITCHCRAFT

Magick and Communication Skills

Emily Carlin

What do communication skills have to do with magick? Quite a lot, in my experience. The way I see it, magick is about understanding exactly what you want to do with your magick and then communicating that intent to the universe in order to manifest it. How can you expect to properly form a spell to get what you want if you cannot clearly articulate what you want? Being able to specify precisely what you desire to the universe is critical to the success of any magickal working.

The first question to ask yourself before any magickal working is: *What is my intent?* What is it that you want your magick to accomplish? Most, if not all, magickal acts have specific goals, such as "help heal my brother's broken arm," "help me find a better job," or "protect me from gossip." These goals are generally stated during the course of the magickal working, whether the statement of intent is verbalized, converted into a sigil, visualized, written on a piece of paper and burned, or expressed using some other method. How well those goals are articulated can have a huge impact on the effectiveness of the magick being done. Yes, some may say that the universe will take care of any ambiguity in your intent, but why put so much effort into your magickal act and then let it fizzle into "whatever the gods will"? The clarity and deliberateness of your intent are what separate magick from prayer. By more clearly understanding and articulating your true intent, you take greater control over your magick and increase its potency.

Before you can effectively communicate your magickal intent, you first need to better understand what that intent really is. Let's look at one of the previous examples: "help heal my brother's broken arm." It seems pretty simple at first glance, but let's look a bit deeper. Why do you want to heal the arm, and how? Is your brother in pain and you want to minimize his suffering even if that slows down the healing? Is he being forced to take time off from work that he can't afford and thus you want to speed his healing even if it makes the process more painful? Are there other medical conditions, like a compromised immune system, being affected by the injury that need to be safeguarded? Are there potential complications you're trying to help him avoid? Even something as outwardly straightforward as healing an injury can have numerous complexities when you look at the totality of the circumstances.

Magickal goals like "protect me from gossip" are even more complex. In that type of situation you need to look at the objective facts of the situation, identify your own motivations, and attempt to surmise the motivations of the other people involved in order to fully explore and clarify your own intent. Let's say that the objective facts of the situation are that you work in a small office and one of your coworkers has a bad habit of saying nasty things about people behind their backs. This could create a lot of different, and potentially conflicting, motivations for doing a protection spell. You might be concerned about being made to look bad in front of your boss or peers, you might be worried about your work environment becoming too stressful, and you might want to punish the gossiper for saying bad things about people.

There are a lot of different magickal acts that can address those motives (protections, bindings, glamours, etc.). How you decide to go about accomplishing your goals should, as much as is feasible, take into account the motivations of the gossiper. You can never really know what someone else is thinking, but thoughtful observation and perhaps an outside opinion or two should give you some insight. Is the person envious of others, seeking attention, looking to make themselves look better by putting others down, or perhaps dealing with pain and stress in an unhealthy way? In this situation your real intent may be to protect your own reputation and working relationships by making your positive contributions outshine any negative gossip headed your way. Alternatively, your real intent might be to improve the general atmosphere in the office by binding the gossiper against doing harm while simultaneously recognizing their positive efforts in order to address their envy and insecurities. By better understanding what you want and how you want to get it, you are more likely to do magick that will actually accomplish those specific goals.

One of the easiest ways to better understand your intent is to write down your immediate goal and then ask yourself why you want it. Write down your answer and then once again ask yourself *why?* Do this until you have as complete a picture of the circumstances and your own motivations as possible. If your goal is to find a better job, ask why you want that. Your answer might be something like, "I need a higher salary and better hours." Why do you want that? "To be able

to afford to go out on occasion and not be so tired when I get home." Why do you want those things? "I want to be able to have fun and enjoy my time off. I want to feel better about my life." You'll know you've dug deep enough into your intent when all of the answers to *why?* are basic physical and emotional needs: food, shelter, security, emotional well-being, etc. In asking why, we've clarified what constitutes "a better job." In this case, the goal really is to find a job that pays a salary high enough to afford a more comfortable lifestyle that isn't as mentally or physically draining and that allows for a more positive general outlook. Magick tends to follow the path of least resistance to a goal, so if we just do a spell for a "better" job, we might get something that pays better but is more stressful and has worse hours, or perhaps something with a flexible schedule and low stress but that barely pays the bills. By doing a magickal working that specifically addresses the needs you're trying to fulfill, you're a lot more likely to get the end result you want than if you do a more vague working.

Now that you better understand what you really want your magick to accomplish, you need to communicate that intent to the universe in order to manifest it. For any preplanned or complex working, I recommend writing a formal statement of intent that explicitly states what you want, why you want it, and how you want to get it.

Now that you better understand what you really want your magick to accomplish, you need to communicate that intent to the universe in order to manifest it.

For any preplanned or complex working, I recommend writing a formal statement of intent that explicitly states what you want, why you want it, and how you want to get it. Take your time with this. Write a draft and put it away for a few days, then come back to it and revise it. Keep revising until you are satisfied that it fully articulates the totality of your intent. If you have other people you work with and are comfortable with them reading your statement of intent, then have them read it and reflect back to you what they think you intend. This is a great way of making sure that what you wrote really makes sense, rather than just having it make sense inside your own head. The more important your working is, the more valuable outside feedback can be. If you don't have a local community you're comfortable working with, there are always online communities, particularly on Facebook and Tumblr, where you can ask people for their input. Once you are satisfied that what you've written down makes sense, you can implement it in your working.

There are many ways to incorporate your complete statement of intent into a working. For some workings, particularly elaborate rituals, it may be appropriate to read your statement of intent aloud as part of the working. For other types of magick, it may be appropriate to read your statement of intent silently while visualizing your goal and putting your energy into it, perhaps then burning the written statement to release the energy you've put into it. A popular way of shortening an elaborate statement of intent is to convert it into a sigil. (There are many works both in print and online that go into making sigils in depth, so I won't cover that here. I recommend *Practical Sigil Magic* by Frater U∴D∴.) Once you have a sigil of your intent, you can carve it into a candle, stitch it on a bag, draw it on paper, etc., and use it to empower a spell or working. You can also meditate on your statement of intent in order to create a symbol, set of movements, combination of herbs, etc., that represents your intent. Use your creativity and

imagination to find the simplification that feels right to you, then charge it with the power of your full intent and do your working.

Having a complete statement of intent, even if it's only for your own understanding, is particularly important for any working involving external entities. Anyone who's ever worked with ancestors, fae, Goetics, spirits, or other metaphysical entities knows that some of them will go out of their way to follow the exact letter of what you've asked of them while purposely subverting your intent—often because they think it's hilarious. Think of the famous "Monkey's Paw" story, where you make a wish and the paw will grant it, but in the most horrible way possible. Working with external entities can feel a lot like that sometimes, though usually less deliberate malevolence is involved. Taking the time and trouble to fully outline not only what you want but also how you want to get it can save you a lot of cleanup later. There are few times when clearly communicating your intent is more important than when working with sentient metaphysical beings.

Of course, there isn't always time to write a full statement of intent. When you're walking out to your car late at night in a dark, deserted parking garage, you don't really have time to analyze why you want to do a protection spell. At times like this, your mind shouting "SAFETY!" at the top of its noncorporeal lungs will do the trick just fine. The purpose of writing a full statement of intent is to maximize the effectiveness of your magick. Most spur-of-the-moment magick is done in reaction to what's happening around you while it's happening. Sure, your knee-jerk reaction is going to be less fully formed and thought out than something more measured, but that's okay. When you need to do spur-of-the-moment magick, do what you feel you need to do and then do a more fully thought-out damage-control working later if you need to. On the plus side, the more often you take the time to fully explore your intent, the more your mind will be trained to think along those lines and the more accurate your in-the-moment thoughts are likely to be. Taking the time to be truly clear about your intent when possible will benefit all of your magickal workings.

Your words and the intent behind them have the power to manifest your will in the world. By deliberately exploring not only your immediate goals but also the underlying needs that are addressed by those goals and the methods by which you'd like to see those goals manifested, you can better understand what you truly want your magick to do. That understanding then allows you to more accurately convey your true intent in your workings. The extra care you put into the thoughts, words, and actions that communicate your intent to the universe allows your magick to manifest your intent more effectively, giving you the results you truly want.

Emily Carlin *is an eclectic Witch, writer, teacher, mediator, and ritual presenter based in Seattle. She currently teaches one-on-one online and at in-person events on the West Coast. For more information and links to her blogs, go to http://about.me/ecarlin.*

Illustrator: Kathleen Edwards

Good Vibe Badass: Positive Strategies for Dealing with Challenging People & Situations

Tess Whitehurst

So you want to be a beacon of love and light but you don't want to attract those who will mistreat you. You'd prefer to be friendly and approachable—maybe even sweet—but you don't want to end up a doormat. You'd really like to see things in the most optimistic way possible, but you really *wouldn't* like to gloss over mistreatment, swallow insults, settle for things that don't feel right, or basically put up with anything that doesn't serve you. You're asking, "Hey, how do I stay positive and deal with challenging people and situations at the same time?" And you want answers.

In short, you want to be a good vibe badass.

In this article, we'll build a solid framework on which to fly the sails of good vibe badassery. In essence, we'll look at how to live every single day in a way that supports positivity, truth speaking, and effective personal boundaries.

It's going to be fun! Are you excited? I am!

Everyday Good Vibeyness (Oh Yay, Another Day!)

First things first: a good vibe badass must cultivate everyday good vibeyness. You probably expected this, but in case you didn't, please note that this is non-negotiable, so don't try to argue. Resistance is futile.

The famed law of attraction (as stated by Abraham-Hicks) says, "That which is like unto itself is drawn." Similarly, the threefold law states, "That which you send out [emotionally, physically, and energetically] comes back to you threefold [in some equal though non-identical form]." So to transform negativity and to attract positive people and situations into your sphere, you absolutely must start with yourself.

If you usually wake up and think sarcastically, "Oh great, here we go," it's important to put in the necessary time and effort so that you instead wake up and think, with a total lack of irony, "Oh yay, another day!" Maybe not in exactly those words, and maybe not every single day, but you'll want to aim for something close.

It's likely that you've read a lot of books on staying positive (there is certainly no shortage of them, some of which I have written myself), so I won't go into too much detail here. Still, because it's such a fundamental key to this whole topic, I would be remiss if I didn't offer at least a couple of simple ideas for how to get and stay in a mainly positive momentum and flow.

So here they are: the first is for the morning and the second is for the evening. Try these for ten days straight and see if you don't manifest far greater harmony and success in your relationships (and every other life area as well).

The Dance Party of One

Author Pam Grout, in her delightful book E *Cubed*, recommends playing a happy song in the morning (among others, she suggests "Celebration" by Kool and the Gang and "I Feel Good" by James Brown), pumping your fist several times, then dancing like you just scored a touchdown.

When your body moves in a happy, joyful, or confident way, your mind and emotions follow very quickly. (If you don't believe me, just try it!) And then, because like attracts like, your outer world magically begins to shape itself according to these purposefully established inner conditions.

So choose a song or a collection of songs that vibrates in a way you immediately recognize as being particularly buoyant and joyful. Then put it on in the morning and dance as ridiculously as you possibly can, thrusting and grinding your pelvis generously and even making yourself laugh if possible.

I am so serious right now. I challenge you to do this faithfully for ten days in a row and NOT feel like life is almost unbearably precious and entertaining.

The "What Went Well" Exercise

Author and renowned psychologist Martin Seligman recommends writing down in the evening three things that went well over the course of your day and why. These things may be seemingly tiny (like drinking a delicious cup of coffee or hearing a great song on the radio), seemingly gigantic (like getting engaged), or anywhere in between. The "why" can be anything that lent itself to the event actually happening. For example, you may have had a delicious cup of coffee because the beans were organic and the water was cold. You may have heard that great song on the radio because you chose to turn on the radio and the DJ chose to play it. And, of course, you may have gotten engaged because your partner asked you and you

said yes. This method is straightforward and clinically proven to be effective. But don't take my word for it—try it! And then try it again, for at least ten days in a row.

Everyday Badassery (Oh Yay, Another Challenge!)

I just typed "badass definition" into Google and found "a tough, uncompromising, or intimidating person" and "a formidably impressive person." Congruently, as an adjective, Google says that *badass* means "tough, uncompromising, or intimidating" or "formidably impressive."

So, yes! That's exactly what we're going to be: good vibe badasses. Our boundaries are going to be light, bright, loving, and tough as nails. We are not going to compromise when it comes to our self-love, authentic expression, and personal freedom. We are going to intimidate the *hell* out of anyone who attempts to bully, mislead, or otherwise mistreat us—not with threats of violence or fear, but with relentless honesty, integrity, and calm inner strength. It won't be our intention to intimidate, but intimidation will be a natural response in anyone with less-than-sterling intentions toward us. And impressive? You'd better believe it is going to be impressive.

Now, all of that may sound spectacular, but how do we actually get there?

Well, first of all, let's consider the badass archetype. Specifically, let's consider *Buffy the Vampire Slayer*. Even if you've never watched this TV show (which you should!), you likely know that the main character is a high school girl in possession of superpowers that allow her to fight and defeat vampires, demons, and all varieties of malevolent creatures. And since she's so good at it, you can tell that she legitimately enjoys it. When a vicious foe appears, even if she is in a most dire situation, she gets a spring in her step and starts lightheartedly bantering as she fights. And when it's been a while since she's come upon any bad guys to fight, she gets restless and wishes something would happen so she could exercise her formidable (badass!) vanquishing abilities. (Finn the Human in the marvelous cartoon *Adventure Time* is another heroic character who actively looks for bad guys to defeat. Extra-credit good-vibe-badass homework: watch both these shows.)

To paraphrase, badassery is the mindset that reacts to challenges with positivity—joy even! You might truly say that when something that needs to be dealt with appears, a badass's subtext would be, "Oh yay, another challenge!"

Here are the things all badasses know:

• Life would be boring and possibly even pointless without challenges.

• Every challenge contains an opportunity.

• Life throws us the challenges that will benefit us most to overcome.

• Even if a situation is difficult or unpleasant in some way, immersing ourselves in it fully will ultimately bring great rewards.

- Nothing is more satisfying than moving out of our comfort zone, even though, by definition, that means experiencing discomfort.

If you're looking at these bulletpoints and thinking that you may not entirely be embodying your inner badass quite yet, don't worry! Like good vibeyness, badassery is a habit, and when you make a point of practicing it, it gets easier and more natural over time.

Positive Self-Regard

I have discovered some serious perils and pitfalls of positive thinking, and one of the major ones is this: the belief that one should be (or at least that one should appear) perfect—spiritually, psychologically, or physically. This is a sure recipe for failure, so if it's somewhere in your consciousness, weed it out! Of course, we all have a shadow of this belief to some extent, but the problem arises when we put a lot of stock in it and actually behave as if it's true.

For example, as a spiritual writer and teacher, I have at times detected surprise when new friends or acquaintances discover that I'm sometimes filled with vitriol or jealousy or that I still have an unhealed wound from the past. Um, yeah, of course I do! Just like every single other human being. If I tried to convince myself or anyone else that I was this totally perfect little spiritual guru with no more lessons to learn, I would not only be full of crap, but also lonely and miserable. As the author Denise Linn often says on her radio show and writes in her books, "The soul loves the truth." Putting on a show of perfection would be gravely insulting to my truth-loving soul.

Similarly, if you feel that you must conceal your challenges from others, or if you're in denial about having any (i.e., if you're concealing them from *yourself*), then you're going to want to change that if you're truly interested in being a badass. After all, as Ana Brett and

Ravi Singh say in their *Warrior Workout* yoga video, "What a warrior fights against is his or her own limitations." How can you fight against your limitations if you're busy putting on a show of not having any?

Let's be clear. I am *not* recommending *in any way* that you beat yourself up for your limitations or imperfections. Quite the contrary! Instead, I recommend that you find them intriguing and exciting. "Oh yay, another challenge!," remember? If, for example, you realize that you're really jealous of a former high school friend because of all the success she appears to be having, you can get a kick out of it. You can think, "Wow, that is interesting! Now why would I feel jealous of someone else's success when it clearly doesn't hamper my ability to experience my own success? Fascinating! Now let's see: what can I learn from this?" Then you might do some journaling and realize that there are some choices this person has made that you wish you had made. Maybe she moved to a city you've always wanted to live in or started a business like one you have fantasized about starting. Once you realize these things, you can act on your newly uncovered desires in some way. It might be scary, but it will be exciting! And you'll find that the more you move toward your own bliss, the more the jealousy will dissipate. Then you'll realize the jealousy wasn't a flaw after all. It was actually a road sign pointing toward your power!

If you dig deep, you can also find hidden caches of power beneath health challenges, sexual blocks, and relationship disharmony. You can see this self-assessment as self-critical drudgery or you can see it as an exciting treasure hunt. It's truly up to you.

If you dig deep, you can also find hidden caches of power beneath health challenges, sexual blocks, and relationship disharmony. You can see this self-assessment as self-critical drudgery or you can see it as an exciting treasure hunt. It's truly up to you.

So, in much the same way the great therapists of the world treat their patients, get in the habit of looking at your own stuff with neutrality and positive self-regard. Don't take anything personally—not even your personal challenges. Living in this way is one of the hallmarks of a true and abiding badass.

When it comes to people who challenge us, quite often they are mirroring back our shadow, or the things within us that we have not yet looked at honestly or made peace with. So it can be very helpful to take a bit of time to ask: *What is it about this person that I have not yet examined within myself? What exactly bothers me about him or her, and is there any conceivable way that I possess these same traits and/or behaviors (or am afraid that I do)? If so, can I admit them, accept them, and surround them in the healing light of awareness and love?*

Again, this isn't self-criticism, it's just good-spirited self-exploration.

Sterling Ethics and Integrity

It's been said that life isn't a fairy tale, but life and fairy tales definitely have some similarities. For example, so often in fairy tales, a decision to behave unfairly or disloyally—even in the tiniest of ways—tends to be the snag in someone's scheme and can be the cause of their ultimate unraveling. Indeed, if you remain in the highest possible integrity in all your dealings—or at least if you do your best to do so—you will be a truly formidable opponent. Your honest assertiveness will be tough to ignore, and all your actions will be underscored by a deep inner knowing that you are, really and truly, in the right. Energetically, integrity is like a strong framework and armor of light. That's why an important aspect of being a badass is holding yourself to the highest possible standards of integrity. (Of course, this isn't always black and white, but when we continually tune in to the divine and the part of us that is one with the divine, we have an inner compass that points us in the direction that feels best to our soul.)

With this in mind, no matter how angry, annoyed, or frightened I get, I do my best to stay meticulously honest and fair and to remain on course with my inner compass. I also do my best to refrain from yelling or being snide or sarcastic, and to maintain a level of respect for the person with whom I am dealing. Do I always succeed? Ha! No, not at all. But I do honestly try, because I know that I'm at my most effective when I don't give away my power through acting defensive or attempting to push others around. And I like to think that I get better at it every time I practice. (See that positive self-regard in action? I'm like, "Atta girl! Keep at it. You'll get there someday.")

Embracing Anger

Now, I don't want to give you the idea that I'm anti-anger. I'm all about feeling angry when anger is appropriate—*all* about it. In fact, I've found that it's best when I stay so in touch with my anger that I never let it build up to a boiling point. That way I can channel it into speaking my truth clearly and firmly every step of the way. You know, like a steam engine instead of a volcano.

Of course, we live in a culture that is very weird about anger, so we mustn't judge ourselves if we *do* unwittingly let it build to a boiling point. The important thing is that, as soon as we notice it, we do what we need to do to express it and get it out of our body and emotions. (This may involve privately hitting a pillow with a tennis racket or screaming your head off in your car before you take necessary action

in the outside world.) Otherwise, in addition to causing challenges in our relationships, this anger can take the form of stress, anxiety, and (eventually) health challenges.

From a neutral evolutionary perspective, anger is great! It's a natural response to unfairness and gets our adrenaline pumping so we can defend ourselves as well as the other people, animals, and causes we care about.

Transmutation

If you hadn't guessed by now, there's no simple answer to the question of how to deal with challenging people and situations. But by keeping your spirits high, approaching every challenge with a sporting attitude, painstakingly remaining in integrity, speaking your truth, and having a healthy relationship with anger, you'll be in the most helpful possible mindset for the ultimate goal of good vibe badassery. And what is that goal? Transmutation: the act of transforming problems into lessons, anger into power, and challenges into blessings.

Transmutation is like fire. Think of how fire takes old, dead wood and transforms it into something bright, moving, warm, and full of energy. Also like fire, transmutation is fed with oxygen, so remember to breathe. Yoga and deep-breathing exercises—as well as simply being conscious of your breath on a moment-to-moment basis—can be excellent complements to your badass efforts and are invaluable for times in your life when you're dealing with a challenging person.

Finally, one of my favorite transmutation tools is to visualize violet fire or lilac-colored flames. If I'm feeling challenging emotions, for example, or thinking negative thoughts, I will fill my mind and body with the visualization of purple fire. I will feel the heat and hear the sound of crackling flames in my mind's eye, and I will set the intention to transform any and all stuck or seemingly unhelpful energies into lightness, brightness, and ideal forward movement. I might also do this with my home or any other interior area, or even the person with whom I am experiencing a challenge. This way, nothing is wasted. Everything is precious fuel for the dynamic fire of my soul's unfolding.

Connected to Everyone with Love

When you're in the midst of a really nasty challenge, sometimes the last thing you want to hear is that old New Age standby: just surround the situation in love. Still, when we remember that our separation from others really is an illusion and that we are, in truth, one with everyone and with All That Is, it can help put the whole thing in perspective. Because ultimately, whatever we're stressing about is not actually as serious and heavy as it seems. In fact, you might say that every drama is actually a karmic game that helps us learn our soul's lessons as best we can. Sure, on one level it all seems real, and it certainly feels real, and it's important that we acknowledge and honor that. But what's *actually* going on here? Love. Underneath the seeming discord, the real good vibe badass knows that at the end of the day that's all there really is. Kind of takes the pressure off, doesn't it?

Tess Whitehurst *is a feng shui consultant, intuitive counselor, and award-winning author. She's also the founder and fascilitator of* The Good Vibe Tribe, *a membership site with online workshops and weekly web chats about magical and spiritual living. Learn about her work and sign up for her free monthly newsletter at www.tesswhitehurst.com.*

Illustrator: Tim Foley

Scent and Sentiment: Diffuse the Healing Properties of Your Favorite Scents

Lexa Olick

Fragrance is a quiet culprit that can easily sneak up on us. It lingers in the air and may even go unnoticed until we're suddenly transported to a different time and place. After we return from our reverie, we realize it was triggered by a familiar smell. While one quick whiff is sometimes powerful enough to reawaken our memories, other times we may catch ourselves sniffing the air repeatedly in order to jog our mind. Even if that memory remains at the tip of our tongue, the feeling is still there inside us. Scents create a comforting atmosphere, so even an act as simple as entering a room can instantly elevate our mood. Grandmother's perfume, a walk in the garden, and freshly cut grass are all common scents that may evoke feelings of nostalgia.

Since scents have the ability to instantly lift our mood, keeping a scent close at hand is beneficial for whenever we may need that boost. However, how we enjoy a scent is just as important. Some sources of fragrance require a flame to release the scent. The act of lighting incense or burning essential oils becomes a visual experience as well as a fragrant one. These visual methods of smoke and flame create atmosphere and set the mood just as scents do. Lit candles and swirling smoke inspire moments of quiet reflection and enhanced concentration. The flicker of a candle also focuses our mind and allows us to target specific energies during a ritual. The warmth of a single flame sets the right tone for meditation.

Unfortunately, there are instances in which we won't be able to use our preferred methods of enjoying fragrances. Certain places, such as dorm rooms, apartments, or offices, may not allow the use of smoke or fire. Luckily, there are other ways to diffuse scents into the air that require little effort.

At the end of this article are instructions for making a diffuser pendant that is easy to use. The folksy pendant is recycled from broken terracotta pots. Because of the pendant's handcrafted nature, each piece will be unique. While most oil diffusers are suitable only for an altar or a table, jewelry is something you can always carry with you wherever you go. Pendants are transportable vessels that can elevate your mood and brighten your wardrobe.

Instead of relying on a flame, these pendants use your own body heat to warm the fragrance of the oils. Since the pendants are recycled from terracotta pots, the clay is already fired. Kiln-fired clay ensures that the pendants can withstand moisture and not crumble when wet, which means they are durable enough to wear every day. Terracotta clay is a material well known for being porous and absorbent. The back of the pendant remains untouched so that it can readily absorb the essential oil of your choice and diffuse the fragrance into the air. As the scent circulates around you, you will be able to enjoy the healing and aromatic benefits of the essential oils wherever possible.

Terracotta pots are generally known as ideal homes for flowers. The pots keep roots protected and are sturdy enough to stand up to wind. Unfortunately, as anyone who happens to garden knows, pots also have a way of breaking, which leaves you to pick up the pieces. Instead of sweeping up the shards and tossing them away, save the broken pots and transform the pieces into art pendants.

For me, there is nothing more grating than a broken terracotta pot. Not only do I mourn the loss of a good flowerpot, but I also cannot bear the unpleasant sound of two ceramic shards scraping against each other. That noise sounds worse than fingernails on a chalkboard. However, with this project, I am able to take something that makes me cringe and turn it into something that makes me smile.

When choosing scents to diffuse, look for authentic essential oils, which are those extracted from natural botanicals. These genuine oils retain some of the plant's magical energies and are therefore more effective in your works. Plus, their fragrance lasts longer and keeps the air around you fresh. Stay away from synthetic oils or blends, because they won't have the same therapeutic or magical properties of the plant or flower. The synthetic fragrances only duplicate a smell.

Diffuser Pendant

To make a diffuser pendant, you will need the following supplies:

- Piece of a broken terracotta pot

- Fine grit sandpaper

- A warm, damp cloth

- Craft acrylic paint

- Paintbrush

- Mini rubber stamp (approximately ¾ inch)

- E6000 permanent craft adhesive (optional)

- Natural stones or shells (optional)

- Brush-on clear acrylic sealer (matte varnish)

- Glue-on flat pad bail

- Chain or cord with clasp (18 inches or longer)

- 1–2 drops essential oil

Step One

Since terracotta pots can break in unusual shapes, try to find a piece that is around an inch in size. There is no wrong size when it comes to creating your own jewelry, but an inch of space allows enough room to attach a bail and still be small enough not to overwhelm your neck. If you can't find a piece small enough, you can take a hammer and very carefully break the pieces into smaller fragments. A larger piece can make for an excellent statement necklace. If you like bold jewelry, you can use a piece that is about two inches in size, or you can even purchase a ready-made two-inch terracotta saucer (available where most pots are sold).

Step Two

Take your sandpaper and gently sand away the rough edges of the broken terracotta piece. The edges are normally not sharp, but sanding the broken edges rounds off the corners and gives it a more finished look that allows the pendant to rest against your skin. Sanding also prevents the clay from crumbling further.

Step Three

Take a warm, damp cloth and gently clean the terracotta piece so it is free from any dust after sanding. I don't recommend using soap because it may leave a slight residue. Let the wet terracotta shard dry completely overnight.

Step Four

Once the terracotta piece is dry, paint only the edges with acrylic paint. It is best to choose a color that matches the color of your bail. If your bail is gold, use gold paint. If your bail is silver, use silver paint. Once the edges are painted, set the terracotta piece aside to dry.

Step Five

The front of the terracotta piece is the side you will decorate. With your brush, apply an even layer of paint to your rubber stamp. I recommend black paint because it has a stronger pigment. Press the stamp onto the front of the terracotta piece. If you are artistic enough, you can paint your own design with a paintbrush by hand or draw your design with a permanent marker. Once the design is complete, set it aside to dry fully.

Alternatively, you can glue natural stones or shells onto the front of the terracotta piece with E6000 adhesive. Cabochons and abalone shells look especially nice with this clay.

Step Six

Apply an even coat of acrylic sealer to the front and sides of the terra-cotta piece. The back needs to remain untouched so it can still absorb the essential oil. Once you have applied the sealer, set it aside to dry. Of course, only painted or drawn designs need a coat of sealer for protection. If you chose to glue stones or shells onto your pendant, don't apply any sealer to the embellishments.

Step Seven

Adhere the bail to the back of the pendant with E6000 adhesive. Glue-on bails are easy to use because they have a flat area that can be attached to nearly any design to create beautiful, finished pieces of art. They make customizing jewelry a breeze because they don't require the use of a drill. Once the glue-on bail is firmly adhered, set the pendant aside to dry.

Step Eight

Thread a chain through the bail so you can wear the necklace around your neck. A black cord especially complements the warm color of the terracotta clay.

Step Nine

Apply one to two drops of essential oil to the back of the pendant. The clay is absorbent, so it will quickly grip the oil and gently diffuse it. A fresh scent will greet you with every move you make and follow you throughout the day. If you use a dark shade of essential oil and worry that it might stain your skin, you can simply wait until the pendant dries before you wear it around your neck.

This project can easily be modified to create a magnet to display on your fridge or other magnetic surfaces. Simply skip the bail and glue a magnet to the back of the clay instead. Just leave enough space of exposed clay on the back of the magnet to apply essential oil. You can also use the pendants as potpourri. By not attaching a bail to the back of the clay, you can easily drop a piece anywhere a fresh scent is needed. All you need is one to freshen a room, but you can gather several in a decorative bowl or sachet for a nicer display.

Lexa Olick *is the author of* Witchy Crafts: 60 Enchanted Projects for the Creative Witch. *She has previously contributed to other almanacs, such as* Llewellyn's 2016 Witches' Companion, 2015 Sabbats Almanac, 2014 Witches' Companion, *and* 2013 Herbal Almanac. *She is a graduate of the University of Buffalo, where she studied art and art history. When she is not writing or crafting, she spends her time traveling, gardening, and adding to her collection of antique glassware. She currently lives in New York with her family and several hyperactive pets.*

Illustrator: Neil Brigham

Speaking with the Gods: Omens in a Modern World

Stephanie Woodfield

It's been one of those days. It feels like I've been running late for everything. My alarm didn't go off in the morning, and I scrambled to get to work on time. One problem after another cropped up at work, and I left an hour later than usual. And because of that I'm both distracted and rushing to get home and change, because the friend I was supposed to meet after work for drinks has been waiting for me for the last twenty minutes, wondering where I am. The narrow roads that lead to my house in Connecticut twist and wind

through the landscape, going up and down hills and valleys. But they are familiar to me, and I know just where to turn. I know the shape of every curve and barely need to think about it as I drive. And I drive a bit on the fast side, just wanting to get home and meet my friend.

Then there is a loud caw and the sweep of black wings as a large crow swoops down and flies in front of my car, its wings brushing the hood. I am both startled and terrified that my car will collide with the crow. My patron goddess is the Morrigan, the Irish personification of battle and sovereignty whose favorite form in her myths is appearing in the shape of a crow or raven. I briefly wonder what happens to you if make your patron deity's favorite animal roadkill. I conclude that it can't be a good thing and slow the car down to a crawl. I'm the only one on the road that I can see, but I also know that the Morrigan is a goddess of prophecy, and she and I have a long-standing agreement about omens. Something isn't right. I need to pay attention.

The next curve goes up a steep hill, and when I get to the top, going five miles below the speed limit, I see a woman frantically trying to push her car to the side of the road. Taking a deep breath, I realize that if I hadn't seen the crow and slowed down, I would have hit the car or the woman, or both. It's the worst possible place for a car to stall and she knows it. I pull over and help the woman push the car onto the grass, shaking a little with the knowledge that I came very close to having a potentially horrible accident. The woman calls a tow truck, her car safely off the road, and when I finally get home, the first thing I do is pour an offering on the Morrigan's altar and breathe a grateful "thank you."

· · · · · · · · · · · · ·

Omens are an everyday part of my life. At times they are things I seek, when I ask a particular question and look for guidance. Other times they are things I do not expect, like the crow flying over my car and making me slow down. But they always end up being exactly what I need at the time, even if I don't know it yet. The majority of the time the Morrigan is referred to as a goddess of battle and sovereignty, but as with any deity, there are many layers to her nature. Seeing the future and delivering warnings and omens to the gods or favored mortals plays heavily in the Morrigan's stories, and today she is no different. You don't have to work with the Morrigan or a deity connected to prophecy to be able to receive omens, but my dedication to her has taught me to look more closely at exactly what omens are and how I can learn to speak with the gods through them.

So what exactly is an omen? How do we know with certainty when we receive one? To put it simply, omens are messages—messages that have specific meaning to us. Most of the time we get very caught up in exactly what the omen we receive means and forget to look at the most basic part of the process. If an omen is a message, then it is coming from somewhere. It could be from an ancestor, a friend or relative who has passed, a spirit, or a god. It's a conversation. It's communication with the unseen at the most basic level. And it's not a one-way conversation, or at least it doesn't have to be.

Omens are simply one of many ways we can communicate with the divine or other beings. We ask questions, and we can set up specific guidelines as to how we receive and recognize messages. In many ways this makes the messages we are given more impactful. If we ask the universe to provide an omen in a very specific way, then when it occurs we are more likely to pay attention to the message. If you have ever used a pendulum, you are familiar with the idea of establishing certain protocols in order to receive a message. You have to set up rules. When the pendulum swings this way it means "yes," and when it swings that way it means "no." When we look at receiving omens as a two-way conversation, we can also set certain boundaries and ask for specific things. We don't have to wait for the universe or the gods to send us messages in random ways. We can set the stage for how we wish the communication to happen.

> **Omens are simply one of many ways we can communicate with the divine or other beings. We ask questions, and we can set up specific guidelines as to how we receive and recognize messages. In many ways this makes the messages we are given more impactful.**

When I started working with the Morrigan, I noticed early on that she would send me messages through her crows. I then became very interested in bird augury and researched different methods used in different cultures. Most of the systems I found were either extremely complicated or very vague. Each culture had its own guidelines and rules for what the different types of birds and their actions meant. Essentially the different cultures had told the gods what kinds of signs they would recognize as being legitimate messages. So I treated bird augury very much like using a pendulum. I specifically asked for crows flying toward the left to indicate a "no" or negative answer or something negative in general and for crows flying toward the right to be "yes" or a positive answer. And when I started asking questions for signs, this was very much how the answers came.

A friend of mine uses what she calls the "rule of three" as her protocol for omens. Whether it's a specific item, symbol, or name being mentioned, when she comes across it or hears it three times, she recognizes it as a sign. Similarly, her sister also has a particular protocol for receiving messages. She asks to find feathers, and will often find feathers crossing her path in unexpected places at just the right time.

What protocols you ask for are up to you. Be as creative as you like. One thing you should consider is whom specifically you are asking for messages. If you ask for guidance or a message from a deity versus an ancestor, you may want to establish specific protocols for each situation. For example, I would not ask to receive a message from the Dagda through crows or bird augury. As one of the Morrigan's sacred animals, the crow makes sense for her. The Dagda tends to help me remember the joy in life and not to take things so seriously. He has a comical side, and messages from him tend to come in the form of laughter or moments when the joke is on me but I can still laugh at myself. If you are asking for a message from a deceased loved one, you may want to choose something that had special meaning to them or makes you think of them. Omens also don't have to be something you receive in the physical realm; they can also be found in dreams, or, if you practice journey work, you can encounter them in the astral realm.

So what happens when you ask a question and all you get is silence? This does happen. Don't be discouraged. This doesn't necessarily mean you did anything wrong. When this happens to me, it's due to one of three things: I'm not asking the right question, I already know the answer, or certain events have to happen before the answer will be clear. When our questions are not clear, it's difficult to get a true answer. Try asking the question in a different way. Don't make it overly complicated; be specific and simplistic if you can. Don't ask open-ended questions.

This may sound obvious, but it's important to recognize that you may already know the answer to your question. When I first started using bird augury, on one occasion I doubted myself and the answer I received to a question and thought, "Well, I see crows all the time. Maybe that was a coincidence." More than likely this was because I hadn't liked the answer. So I asked my question a second time, specifically asking for a second omen to confirm the first. Well, I went from seeing crows all over the place to seeing none whatsoever—not in trees, not anywhere I drove—for about a week. Then when I finally did see a crow, it confirmed the answer I had been given previously. It was like the Morrigan was tapping her

foot and saying, "Oh, so you don't believe me, huh?" She had already given me an answer. I just hadn't trusted it.

There are also times when your question can't be answered yet. While I think there are some things in life that are just meant to happen, I still very much believe in free will. Our choices influence our future, and that future is an ever-changing thing. Sometimes if certain events or choices haven't happened or been made yet, there may be no clear answer to your question. This can be frustrating. If my question is met with silence, then I may shelve the question for a while and ask it again after some time has passed.

While we can set certain protocols for receiving omens, there are times when we will receive messages even though we haven't asked a question, such as when the crow flew in front of my car. It followed the protocol I had set up, but I hadn't asked a question. I wouldn't have known to ask a question in the first place since it was a situation I was unaware of. When you open yourself up to the universe and the gods and they know you are listening, they will start speaking to you. When omens come to us in this manner, they are usually things that are hard to ignore or explain away.

When a friend of mine and I were creating rituals for a retreat honoring the Morrigan, we were discussing certain ideas over the phone. We felt a little stuck and were not sure what direction to go in. As we talked about one particular course of action, I heard a crow call out as it passed by the window I was sitting next to. Then I heard another crow call, this time through the phone's speakers. My friend and I were stunned. We had both heard the two crow calls, moments apart, and on top of that it was also the middle of the night. Crows aren't active after nightfall, and that was the only time I'd ever heard one after dark. We both recognized it as a message and went with the idea we had been talking about when the crows put their two cents in.

So the next time you want to receive a message from the gods or spirits, don't pull out your tarot cards. Wherever you are (in your car, in front of your altar, etc.), take a deep breath, pose your question to the gods, and tell them in what manner you want them to respond. You may be surprised at how quickly they answer.

Stephanie Woodfield *is the author of* Celtic Lore & Spellcraft of the Dark Goddess: Invoking the Morrigan *and* Drawing Down the Sun: Rekindle the Magick of the Solar Goddesses. *Stephanie has been a practicing Witch and Priestess of the Morrigan for over sixteen years. Her articles have appeared in* SageWoman *magazine and* The Portal *and on the* Witches' Voice *website. She is one of the founding members of* Morrigu's Daughters, *an online sisterhood dedicated to the Morrigan. Visit her blog,* Dark Goddess Musings, *at http://darkgoddessmusings.blogspot.com.*

Illustrator: Jennifer Hewitson

The Witchy Household

Cassius Sparrow

Imagine if we could get the same instant gratification from Witchcraft that we see in movies and books! How many of us would incorporate magic into our everyday mundane chores? Laundry done and folded in a flash. Carpets that vacuum themselves, dishes that wash themselves, and beds made with the flick of a wrist. While such things are (currently) impossible, we Witches can incorporate our craft into our everyday tasks.

Clean with Purpose

When you think of cleansing spells, the first thing that probably comes to mind is a long list of spells to perform before and after you work a large magical undertaking, such as personal cleansings, spatial cleansings, altar and workspace cleansings, and cleansing baths. But what about the rest of your home? Why wait until the energy in an area becomes noticeably dirty before tackling the mess?

You can create your own cleaning supplies with a magical twist to replace your chemical-laden, store-bought products. Start with a base of white vinegar and distilled water, and add herbs that correspond to the attributes you want to charm your household. Gardenia petals, juniper berries, mint leaves, and lavender can be added to a vinegar-water base and used as a replacement for air-freshening sprays while adding an element of protection and peace to any room. Lemon peel, rosemary, and garden sage can be added to vinegar-based floor wash to drive away both dirt and negativity, and it smells divine. Cinnamon, sea salt, and orange peel added to a vinegar-water base make an excellent wash for windowsills, doorways, and other thresholds to maintain harmony in the home and keep out malicious energies.

Enchant your broom with cleansing intent for when you sweep. Visualize all the negative things being swept out of your home with

the rest of the dirt and dust. If you have carpets in your home, draw sigils or write charms on your vacuum. Open all the windows to let in fresh air, and call out to prosperity and blessing, inviting them into your home. Hang sachets of herb and flower blends in rooms that need an extra boost. Chant for positivity while you dust, and visualize blessings (rather than the dust) settling over you and your home.

Organize with Intent

We've all done it. We set something down for just a moment and lose it immediately, or we drop something in a drawer only to never see it again. The next time you decide to reorganize everything in your home, consider adding some Witchcraft to this effort.

Paint a sigil for safekeeping on the bottom of your clutter drawer and chant, "Whatever I place in here will always be found when it is needed." Buy or make a little key rack and do the same for it, with the added charm, "I will always remember to hang my keys here," though this may not work for the rest of your family!

Set aside areas in your home for your magical tools. Many Witches have a separate area for doing Witchcraft, such as a workspace or an altar. Maintaining these areas is very important, of course, but where do your tools go when you're done with them? How much time do you spend looking for the things you need for magical workings? It may be time to make a sort of broom closet for your tools. This could be a drawer, a cabinet, a tool box, or even an actual closet. Use sigils for protection and success, make sure everything has a place, and charm both the broom closet and yourself so you will remember to put away your tools when you have completed your work.

Organize your bookshelves and try to keep all your Witchcraft-related books in one place for easy reference. Sort them by subject. Enchant your books with personal, witchy bookplates so that any book lended will always find its way back to you.

Make Magic in the Kitchen

Kitchen Witches have been working Witchcraft into meals for years, but even the most casual Witch can find ways to make dinner more magical. Put together a reference book of the magical properties of common kitchen herbs, then add them to your wishes with purpose and intent. Plan a weekly magical meal. Turn a favorite spell into a dish at dinner. Write your own spells around family recipes. Brew "potions" of teas, lemonades, and mixed alcoholic drinks. Bake breads for prosperity, cakes for harmony, and cookies for wishes and good luck. There's no limit to the amount of Witchcraft you can do with food.

Consider growing and drying your own herbs. The most common witchy herbs are lavender, rosemary, basil, mint, sage, and thyme. All of these thrive well in small container gardens and are easy to dry at home. They are also cost-efficient. Nothing evokes the idea of a

Witch's craft more than the image of bundles of herbs drying in sunny windows. Even the act of growing the herbs can be a spell in and of itself. Paint sigils on the flowerpots and speak charms and petitions to the seeds to grow money, luck, and happiness as they grow themselves.

Bless your kitchen utensils so they never will break or rust. Charm your stove to never burn your meals. Enchant your pantry so it is always full of good things that are easy to find. Whisper the wishes you have for each day to the sugar you stir into your coffee or tea. Pin banishing charms to your fridge to prevent late-night snacking. Keep an LED candle "burning" above your stove to remind you that the kitchen is the hearth of the home and nothing brings people together better than good food.

Get the Family Involved

A complete witchy household has all members of the family involved in the process. Include your significant other and children in the cleaning chores, and show them how to make them more magical in little ways. Teach them your witchy organizational ways and explain the importance and significance of your sigils and charms. Have them suggest their own ideas about working more Witchcraft into the everyday parts of running a household. A home is like a clockwork machine, where every person plays a role to keep the gears turning. With everyone involved, changes to a magical household are more likely to stick, and any changes that don't work can be addressed quickly.

Let's Take This Outside

The outside of a Witch's house is just as important as the inside, and there are plenty of ways to add magical flair no matter where you live.

To create a magical welcome mat, start with a mat you either made yourself or bought. Then enchant it to bless your guests but also to banish and bind anyone who comes to your door with ill intent toward you and your family. Paint wooden signs with sigils for wealth, peace, or any other blessing. Speak your wishes and blessings aloud, and paint the words onto the signs as well. Hang them on your front and back doors, or put them on stakes and plant them in your yard. If you live in an apartment, copy your spell directly on your doors with chalk or essential oils diluted in water. You'll know they are there, but strict landlords and nosy neighbors will be none the wiser.

If you have space for a proper garden, you can turn a corner of your yard into a large Witch's herb garden. Add herbs such as bee balm, lemon verbena, chives, dill, and catnip to the basic botanicals mentioned earlier, all of which are versatile in spells and most of which are excellent additions to recipes. Be sure to do research before you start planting witchy plants so you know which ones are poisonous. If you have children or pets, you might want to reconsider including poisonous plants in your garden unless you are absolutely sure they cannot access it. Turn your flowerbeds into a spell of their own, depending on which flowers you plant. Begonias and petunias are excellent for protection, roses promote love and happiness, and violets are symbols of healing and cleansing. If you are so inclined, you could even turn your yard into a welcoming garden for fairies by planting fairy-friendly plants such as thistle, roses, peonies, and holly. If you have the space for fairy-friendly trees, apple, ash, and oak are favorites of the fae.

There are many wonderful ways to make your home look and feel more witchy, just by making small changes to your usual daily routine. Incorporating Witchcraft into chores and the mundane running of the household is a great way not only to break the monotony but also to help your household become more efficient. Charm and enchant your neighbors and make your home the envy of the neighborhood!

Cassius Sparrow *is a Hellenic Polytheist, Witch, tarot reader, and author. He is a devotee of Hermes and has been a practicing Pagan for over ten years. He currently lives on the Gulf Coast of Florida with his darling wife and their cat, Zucca. In his free time, he can be found writing, baking, or working in his herb garden. Contact him at cassiussparrow@gmail.com.*

Illustrator: Kathleen Edwards

Magickal Reboot

Charlynn Walls

You may remember your first steps down your spiritual path. There was probably a sense of awe and wonder that made your spirit soar, and you may have begun studies that sent your thought processes into overdrive. Initiatory experiences quite probably left you feeling more connected than ever to the divine. You may have even gone so far as to have been dedicated to your path or initiated into a group to cement your commitment.

However, there are times when we become disillusioned with the community, the divine, or even our own self-concept. It might have to do with the death of a family member, a disconnect within the spiritual community, or a personal trial that has left us devastated and questioning our spirituality. What do we do when we reach that crossroads where we face the choice of attempting to reconnect to the magick or just walking a different path?

There are many ways that we can realign our spirit and perform a magickal reboot. Each individual will find a way that resonates with them at the time. We may need to dig in and become more active in the practice of our craft. In order to do so, we may choose to create ritual items for our personal use, start performing daily devotionals to reconnect to the divine, or rededicate ourselves to our path.

Creation of Ritual Items

Taking the time to carefully evaluate which ritual items you would like to add to your own personal supply of tools and which ones you could create yourself enables you to take stock of the aspects of ritual or spell work that appeal to you. It also allows you to decide which aspects you would like to implement on a consistent basis in your practice.

Creating your own ritual items imbues them with your own personal power and establishes an energetic connection between the tools you utilize and your higher self. Throughout the creation process you are actively working on your spirituality in order to generate a physical manifestation of your ideal tool, be it a wand, an altar tile, a staff, an athame, or another item.

You choose the materials, the design, and the method of creation. Once the item is created to your specifications, you can then cleanse and consecrate it for ritual use. I personally have found great fulfillment in working with different materials to create wands and altar tiles. The process in and of itself is cathartic. I choose the materials, such as wood and gemstones, and combine them in various

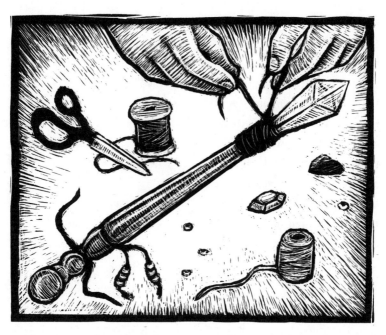

combinations. There have been times when I simply could not get a stone to work in a design the way I originally intended and was forced to alter the concept. Often it ended up turning out better than how I initially conceptualized it. This is an excellent reminder that despite what I may think needs to be done, there are times when my best ideas do not turn out as planned, but if I trust in deity, things often have a way of working out.

Daily Devotionals

Creating a daily routine of active magickal practice can provide a weary heart with a way to reconnect to the divine. This process allows you to make your spirituality a priority. It also requires you to take an active part in it. By becoming more mindful of the approach we take in our daily lives, we can connect to the magickal energies that surround us.

Meditation

I am a very active individual and have a difficult time stopping to relax. When I do force myself to slow down and become mindful of my spiritual practice, I find myself more fulfilled and more at ease.

I write my own guided meditations to help me focus on a specific issue or time of year. A guided meditation allows me to focus on my own voice or a rhythmic beat that shifts my consciousness into a trancelike state. By doing so, I honor what is in my head and heart and let myself connect to those energies.

I often take just five minutes a day to quiet my mind and refocus myself. The meditative process can take place at any time of day and can fit into any busy schedule.

Greet the Day

In addition to simply trying to find a moment for quiet contemplation, there are times when I need to include movement because my grief or anxiety will not allow me to sit still for any length of time or to shut off my brain. A perfect example is when my grandmother passed away. I could not sleep and had difficulty eating, and my mind raced in circles. I was still pretty new to my path and found myself struggling with the concept of death.

I found that by greeting the day each morning, I was able to reconnect to the natural world. This new spiritual practice gave me a way to focus and get on with the business of living. Each morning I was up a bit before sunrise in order to get ready. As the sun rose, it would enter my room and I would stand in the God pose as the sun's rays washed over me.

Standing there with my palms facing upward and my feet firmly planted shoulder width apart, I was able to drink in the sun and recharge my otherwise depleted reservoir of energy. As I stood there taking in deep breaths, I would say the following chant to myself: *Energy of the sun from where I begin, regain and restore balance from within.* I would repeat the chant until I felt sufficiently energetic and connected to the day's energies.

As human beings, we can become disillusioned with our connection to the divine. We want to be heard and recognized. One way we can do that is to ask for guidance from deity. It could be a general affirmation to the God or the Goddess or a specific intention.

In today's modern society, there seems to be a need for instant gratification. Even though we may not be able to receive an immediate answer, just the act of working directly with deity is rewarding. It allows for our own personal expression of emotion.

One way that I like to send out my requests is to write them down. This gives weight to my words and lets them set firmly in my mind. Once I have my request or affirmation composed, I take the paper and place it in a cauldron or other fireproof vessel, then set it on fire. I can see my request being carried up to deity on plumes of smoke. This is a simple yet effective way to remain connected and engaged in the spiritual process.

Rededication

We are often faced with difficult choices along our path. Do we take the most direct route, or do we take the one that may be more rewarding because it provides a challenge that will allow us to grow? When we face such a trial, a rededication to our path can provide us with a new sense of purpose and direction.

I hit a particularly rough patch where I contemplated walking a different path because I had moved away from all of my brothers and sisters in the Craft. I had not been to ritual with them in several months and was feeling particularly disconnected from community and from my own spirituality. It was and still is difficult to put into words how disheartening the situation was.

Although it would have been difficult to make it to all of the gatherings being held over a hundred miles from my home, I rededicated myself to my coven and my path. I decided to renew my vows of commitment to the old gods and to my craft, which I consecrated through a rededication rite. I promised myself I would make the time to travel to our regularly scheduled meetings, I would take time to go to community events that I felt would help bolster my spirituality, and I would make time to reconnect with my spiritual guides and personal deities. Though no one else was there to witness my rededication, it was more to renew my own sense of spirit and connection.

Creating Your Own Rededication Ritual

For your own personal rededication ritual, you will want to include items that you have created yourself, that you have gathered, or that have great personal meaning to you. For my own rededication, I included a wand and an altar tile I had crafted, along with full moon water I gathered. I also included my coven necklace, a black and a white candle, an offering bowl, and a Goddess statue that I had acquired at my first Pagan event.

Arrange the altar in a way that takes into account the cardinal directions and that will allow for your own comfort, as you will want to be able to spend the time needed within the circle. Cast the circle and call the quarters in a way that is in alignment with your path.

When you are ready, you can invite deity into your circle. I chose to invite my patron goddess into my circle. You can do the same, or you can keep it simple and simply refer to the God and Goddess. It would be appropriate to light your candles and incense at this time.

I also placed my coven necklace in my offering bowl and anointed it with a few drops of the full moon water.

When you are ready, you can say your affirmation of rededication to deity. It may reflect the dedication or initiation you have already completed, or it may be a variation on the five-fold kiss,

where you acknowledge specific attributes that will enhance your ability to walk your path. My own affirmation included aspects of my training where I recited the Charge of the Goddess and restated my oaths to honor the old gods and the ways of the Craft, which included *To Know, To Will, To Dare,* and *To Be Silent.* As I made each oath, I anointed my forehead, heart, hands, and mouth with the full moon water. No matter what you include in your affirmation, make sure that what you acknowledge and take as an oath resonates deeply within you and that you will be able to live up to what you are pledging. The gods will take you at your word and will hold you to it.

After saying my affirmation, I sat in quiet contemplation for a while in order to absorb the weight of my vows and to meditate on them. This may be a time when you receive personal messages that will help you along your path. Take note of anything that happens during this rite so you can contemplate what the implications may be later on. When you are ready, thank deity for witnessing your rite and acknowledging your recommitment to your path. You can then release the quarters and close the circle. I chose to leave my altar up for one full cycle of the moon so I would have a visual reminder of promises made.

Anyone can have a crisis of faith that shakes them and makes them reconsider their personal beliefs and needs. How we respond to the crisis will affect how our magickal/spiritual life will be impacted. We can allow ourselves to be victims of circumstance, or we can get back to some very basic concepts and reconnect with our spiritual self, with our communities, and with deity.

By taking the time to create magickal items, perform daily devotionals, and rededicate ourselves, we take an active role in our spiritual lives. By taking responsibility for our actions, we are able to reboot our systems and reaffirm our spirituality in a mindful practice that will sustain us throughout the years to come.

Charlynn Walls *resides with her family in central Missouri. She holds a BA in anthropology, with an emphasis in archaeology. She is acting CEO of Correllian Education Ministries, which oversees Witch School. She is an active member of the St. Louis Pagan community and is part of a local area coven. Charlynn teaches by presenting at various local festivals on a variety of topics. She continues to pursue her writing through articles for* Witches & Pagans *magazine, several Llewellyn annuals, and her blog,* Sage Offerings, *at www.sageofferings.net.*

Illustrator: Bri Hermanson

Witchcraft Essentials

PRACTICES, RITUALS & SPELLS

Music for Ritual and Magic

Peg Aloi

Music can inflame the mind, empower the spirit, and heal the heart. Many practitioners use music to enhance magical workings and ritual work. This article will explore the many uses of music for magical work and suggest some specific artists, recordings, and genres to help enrich your practice.

Music as a component of ritual has a number of different functions. It can be used to set the mood before the rite begins and during the rite itself as energy shifts and different events take place. It can help inspire and accompany movement. It can add drama to a particular piece of performance, such as an enactment of a mystery play or a harvest rite. It can help raise the energy to a more heightened pitch, or calm the energy for more meditative moments. Choosing the appropriate music for use in ritual can greatly enhance the experience for all practitioners.

Think of moments in your life when you remember music playing, whether live or recorded. Chances are those memories include a social ritual of some kind, such as a wedding ceremony, a funeral, or an event honoring an achievement. Music is frequently also a way to mark occasions of victory or celebration, like the parties and receptions that follow more solemn ceremonies, and some songs become well-known theme music for clubs, sports teams, or other groups. Maybe you feel wistful when the radio plays a song that was special to you and a lover, or one that accompanied a deeply emotional time, such as the beginning or ending of a romance. Pagans are often very sensitive to the emotional associations of music, so the use of music in ritual can not only create powerful memories but also elevate our spiritual practice and imbue it with richness.

Pagans are often very sensitive to the emotional associations of music, so the use of music in ritual can not only create powerful memories but also elevate our spiritual practice and imbue it with richness.

When working in a group setting, it is a good idea to have one person responsible for the music, making sure the volume level is appropriate and the music is cued to begin at the right time, and any other technical considerations. The speakers should be placed where they won't be in the way or too loud for anyone standing or sitting near them. MP3 players or iPod

docking stations have built-in speakers, but you can also get small separate speakers that can be placed discreetly on a shelf or table or in a corner. These are very convenient to use because you can create a custom playlist on them beforehand. Sad to say, most people do not use "mix tapes" anymore, but there are some die-hards out there who are still using this ancient technology! CDs can also be used, and a custom playlist can be recorded or burned beforehand.

Those of us who have been in the Pagan community a long time remember the days before the iPod when people collected music on CDs, and before that, cassette tapes, and before that, vinyl records! Cassettes allowed us to mix and match album tracks and record from the radio, giving us the freedom to put anything in a particular order. The mix-tape approach is particularly useful for ritual because we can control the timing of when the music plays to accompany specific moments. Nowadays, burning a CD or creating a playlist on iTunes takes the place of creating a cassette tape. Newer technologies make collecting and recording music much faster and easier.

But let's return to the "good old days" for a moment. In the 1980s, when the Pagan movement was really starting to gain popularity, many covens and individuals used an eclectic assortment of music for their rituals, but the same music would turn up frequently among people in the community. Some music came from the 1970s. The soundtrack to the 1973 film *The Wicker Man* was popular (it contained both songs with lyrics and great instrumental pieces), although it was hard to obtain unless one recorded it from a TV broadcast. Another film soundtrack that many liked to use in ritual, odd as it sounds, was Mike Oldfield's "Tubular Bells," which was used in the 1973 film *The Exorcist*. Some people used Gregorian chant, which can be very atmospheric. One contemporary group with all women performing a cappella is Anonymous 4; their Christmas album *On Yoolis Night* is wonderful and provides some excellent choices to be used in Yuletide rituals.

English folk music, with musicians like Steeleye Span, Pentangle, and Donovan ("Season of the Witch," anyone?), was popular with many Pagans in the 1980s. Traditional music from the other Celtic countries was also a popular choice, and this popularity grew as the Irish music revival swelled through the 1990s with shows like *Riverdance* and bands like Solas and Altan becoming popular in the United States. The instrumental music of John Renbourn (a founding member of Pentangle) is still used by my coven, particularly tracks from his excellent album *The Lady and the Unicorn*. Guitar, mandolin, flute, and other traditional instruments combined through Renbourn's unique arranging style create a sound that is somehow both old and new. Celtic harp music is also very appropriate for ritual use; Alan Stivell is another artist whose work is on some of my coven's ritual tapes.

As Paganism merged with the New Age movement, a lot of music arose that was very suitable for ritual (and was widely imitated).

Some of this music was very meditative, but some of it was more upbeat, incorporating various types of drums and percussion instruments. Gabrielle Roth was one artist whose work was widely used in ritual and still is by many. The appealing sounds from this kind of music later merged with other genres (such as Celtic and African, like the group Afro-Celt Sound System performs) and created whole new hybrid sounds, and these are now popularly used in ritual settings. The harp music of Andreas Vollenweider became popular in the mainstream culture of the 1980s, and some of it was heard in ritual use; the rhythmic string sounds accompanied by flute provided an upbeat but sometimes mysterious accompaniment to magical workings.

So far I've mainly mentioned music that is not necessarily intended to have any kind of Pagan association and yet can prove useful for ritual and magical use, but there is also a great deal of music that incorporates Pagan imagery, lyrics, and themes. Some artists even wrote songs ideal for use as ritual invocations, like Julie Felix's songs from the late 1960s and early 1970s; my coven uses her songs "Clotho's Web" and "Fire, Water, Earth & Air" (from a 1972 album) to this day for every circle casting. There can be no doubt that these songs were intended to accompany Wiccan rites back in the day! Some albums inspire love and devotion due to their Pagan sensibilities, such as Jethro Tull's *Songs from the Wood*. More contemporary music by artists such as Loreena McKennitt are also well loved; songs like "All Souls Night" from her album *The Visit* make fans curious as to the artist's own spiritual leanings.

How to Create an Effective Ritual Playlist

Most rituals begin with creating a sacred space. So when crafting your playlist, you should consider the order in which events occur and the relative timing of those events. It may be that the timing of your working could organically evolve to fit the chosen music as well.

Instrumental music is perhaps best for a ritual circle casting if words are spoken to cast the circle. If music with lyrics is used, it should be played softly enough that the words do not distract from the spoken-word elements. An exception to this is when the participants wish to sing along with the lyrics (as my coven does with Julie Felix's songs); this can be a powerful magical working and can also take the place of other invocations. Contemporary rock artist Ginger Doss (formerly of the bands Velvet Hammer and Dream Trybe) has an upbeat song on her *From Love to Love* album called "Urban Elements" that goes through the elements in order, beginning with fire. I've always thought this would make a perfect invocation accompaniment. A song with an instrumental opening followed by lyrics could work too, such as Loreena McKennitt's "The Mystic's Dream."

The energy of the songs you choose may be related to their tempo and instrumentation. Faster songs tend to create more energy; songs with percussion and complex arrangements are also higher-energy than those with fewer instruments. One reason I enjoy John Renbourn's *The Lady and the Unicorn* is that the instruments used on this album's arrangements (guitar, flute, fiddle) seem to blend seamlessly together to create a sound that is very evocative and also not too distracting. Some instruments have a unique sound that may be appealing for various reasons; many Pagans enjoy drumming of different cultures (like African or Middle Eastern) and unusual instruments like the didgeridoo, which originated in Australia.

One good way to determine the order of songs you choose for your playlist is to chart out the general structure and timing of your ritual, and choose music that will create a natural beginning, middle, and end, following the action of the ritual content. If there is a portion of your rite similar to a mystery play (like a harvest rite, for example), you should probably use instrumental music, unless you choose something with words particular to the ritual action. In that case, the music can actually stand in for any spoken-word activity.

One good way to determine the order of songs you choose for your playlist is to chart out the general structure and timing of your ritual, and choose music that will create a natural beginning, middle, and end, following the action of the ritual content.

The ending portion of a ritual is usually celebratory, as cakes and wine are shared. During this portion, my coven often has John Renbourn's instrumental version of "My Johnny Was a Shoemaker" playing, which has a beautiful melody and slightly upbeat feel. Loreena McKennitt's "Bonny Swans" is also upbeat and beautiful. Some ritual moments are more about the feeling the music can convey than what the lyrics are describing, but lyrics can convey a great deal of potent magical material as well.

Songs for Pagan Festivals

Unexpected musical choices can be very effective for ritual use. Creativity is the key here. Using harvest rituals again as an example, many English folk songs refer to the harvest, to fields of barley, and even to Pagan festivals. Jethro Tull's *Songs from the Wood* album contains many beautiful lyrics celebrating the natural beauty of the English countryside. For example, "Ring Out Solstice Bells" is a nice one for Yuletide. "Cup of Wonder" specifically refers to May Day, as well as ley lines, which are geographic paths of energy in the ancient landscape that connect stone circles and other sacred landmarks.

There are a surprising number of songs that are specific to Pagan festival days or seasons. English singer Steve Ashley sings a lovely song called the "Candlemas Carol" and one called "Fire and Wine"; both are appropriate to the winter season, as is the lilting, lyrical song "Midwinter" by the English folk band Magna Carta. For Samhain, the aforementioned "All Souls Night" by Loreena McKennitt is a great choice, as is her song from an earlier album called "Samhain Night." McKennitt is a perennial favorite with Pagans. Some of her instrumental work is just as evocative as the songs with lyrics, like the "Huron 'Beltane' Fire Dance." For other holidays, such as Litha (summer solstice) or Mabon (autumn equinox), songs that describe the beauty of the natural world are appropriate. Robert Burns's "Westlin Winds" describes the autumn landscape and has been recorded by a number of great artists including Dick Gaughan. Jethro Tull's "Summerday Sands" might be nice for Litha, and it has a pleasing waltz tempo. And don't neglect the rock and roll classics! "Hot Fun in the Summertime" by Sly and the Family Stone is a great choice for Litha, too.

Playlist

Albums

Jethro Tull: *Songs from the Wood, Heavy Horses, Christmas Album*

Loreena McKennitt: *The Visit, Elemental, To Drive the Cold Winter Away*

John Renbourn: *The Lady and the Unicorn, A Maid in Bedlam*

Dead Can Dance: *Into the Labyrinth, Spiritchaser*

British Folk

Donovan, Lal Waterson, The Incredible String Band, Owen Hand

Celtic Artists

Altan, Solas, Karan Casey, Cran, Capercaillie

Drums

Gabrielle Roth

Film Soundtracks

The Wicker Man, The Last Temptation of Christ, Excalibur

Pagan Artists

Kellianna, Incubus Succubus, Ginger Doss, Julie Felix

Psychedelic Rock

The Moody Blues, Jefferson Airplane, Spirogyra, Trees

Scandinavian

Värttinä (*iki*), Garmarna (*Vengeance, God's Musicians*)

Seasonal Songs

"Midwinter" by Magna Carta, "Candlemas Carol" by Steve Ashley, "Forever Autumn" by Justin Hayward

Peg Aloi *is a media studies scholar, writer, singer, and professional gardener. She was the Media Coordinator for* The Witches' Voice *from 1997 through 2008. Her blog,* The Witching Hour (*www.patheos.com/blogs /themediawitches*), *focuses on Paganism and media. With her writing partner, Hannah Johnston, Peg co-organized two academic conferences at Harvard University on Paganism and the media.*

Illustrator: Tim Foley

Circle Games

James Kambos

Belonging to a magical group or a coven can be exciting. The support you can find by belonging to a magical group is amazing, especially during a time of crisis. But working and performing magic is hard work. There must be a feeling of trust and friendship among members of your group for things to run smoothly. Whether you're deciding when to meet or choosing a magical goal, a strong bond must exist between members of the group.

I've found that adding a few activities or games to a meeting or a magic circle can create a feeling of trust and

friendship among members of a magical group. These activities I'm about to share with you aren't meant to dilute or diminish the seriousness of your magical work. Instead, they're meant to lighten the mood, if needed, and to put group members at ease. This should help the magic flow. Besides, some of these activities may help you learn something about a member that perhaps you didn't know. These games and activities can also break the ice if you're new to a group.

I've tried to split these activities into two groups. Some may be used at the beginning of a magic circle. Some may be used at the end of the magic circle after a ritual has been performed. Or you may want to use them after the circle has been cleared and members are socializing.

Participating in any of these activities should be completely voluntary. No one should feel pressured and it's perfectly okay to say, "I'll pass."

I hope you enjoy these circle games and they become a regular part of your magic circle. Some of the activities may seem simple or lighthearted, but they can help to improve concentration and visualization skills—both of which are needed for successful magic.

Greeting Games

These activities can be used at the beginning of a meeting, at the start of a magic circle, or any time you need a get-to-know-you type of activity. You can expand on them or change them to fit your group's needs. I'm sharing them because I've seen them used and they work.

Name That Deity

Almost everyone has a favorite goddess/god or even a guardian angel/spirit that they identify with. For this activity, the group leader will begin by naming their favorite deity. Then the leader will allow up to three members to ask questions about that deity. Questions could be things like: What attracted you to this deity? How do you connect with this deity? Does this goddess/god remind you of yourself somehow? Continue around the circle until everyone has had a chance to participate.

I've Got a Secret

For this activity, hand out blank index cards to everyone. Have each person write something about themselves that they'd like to share. Try to make it something not everyone else knows about, and make it specific. It could be a magical talent you have, or it could be about your pets and their names or perhaps a sport you enjoy. When you're done, don't sign your name. Let the group leader collect them and read each one aloud. Give the group three chances to guess who it is. If no one guesses correctly, then the person whose card it is will raise their hand before the leader reads the next card. This is a great ice breaker for a new group.

MEMORY GAME

This game requires each person to pay close attention. It can help anyone develop better concentration and visualization techniques. To begin, the leader will make a statement that everyone else in the circle can add on to, until the statement is long. Here's an example:

Leader: "I'm going to a sabbat meeting and I'm going to bring incense."

Person 2: "I'm going to a sabbat meeting and I'm going to bring incense and candles."

Person 3: "I'm going to a sabbat meeting and I'm going to bring incense, candles, and a cauldron."

The idea is that not only does everyone need to remember what the people before them say, but they also need to add something new to the sentence quickly. This should be fun, even silly. Going back to the example I used, if someone wants to add "a bag of potato chips," that's okay. If someone gets stuck and doesn't remember what someone said earlier (like me), use pantomime to give them a clue.

Here are some other ideas to get you started:

"I'm going camping and I'm going to bring…"

"I'm going to a party and I'm going to bring…"

"I'm going to a handfasting and I'm going to bring…"

Once you get started, this activity goes quickly and usually gets some laughs.

Activities to Close a Circle

Rituals and the magic that takes place in a magic circle can be exhausting. That is why I feel that any ending activities should be simple and lighthearted. If you choose to end a magic circle with any type of activity, all participants should be allowed to cool down and relax. In some ways, closing activities for a magic circle might be more important than greeting activities. The reason I say this is because, as magic is created during a ritual, many group members may enter an altered state of awareness. An activity at the closing of a magic circle will prepare everyone for getting back to the everyday physical realm. But in some cases, there will be times when you may want to close and clear your magical space first, then have an activity planned for the social time after your circle.

Here are a few ending activities for you to consider.

Roses and Thorns

This activity will allow everyone to share something that made them smile and something that may have ticked them off. Whatever group members share, it should be something that happened that day or that week. Begin by going around the circle and having each person share their "rose" story. Encourage questions and comments: "Why did you enjoy this?" and so on. Next, let everyone share a "thorn" story about something that has peeved them. And again, let others make comments and suggestions as to how the problem could be resolved or avoided, magically or mundanely.

Mini Tarot Readings

You probably have at least one person in your group who is good at giving tarot readings and enjoys it too. This is a fun way to end a magic circle or coven meeting. For this quick read, I prefer to use only the major arcana cards of the deck. Let the reader sit across from anyone who wants a reading. I call the person on the receiving end the "seeker." The seeker will shuffle the cards while concentrating on a question of immediate concern. The seeker will draw one card and lay it down. Then the reader will give a quick interpretation before moving to the next person.

For a variation of this activity, you may use a pendulum instead of the tarot. In this case, allow each person to ask one yes-or-no question.

Giving Thanks

There is no better time or place to give thanks and to show and share your gratitude than at the closing of a magic circle. Showing and saying how thankful you are about something in your life will always have a positive effect on your life and magic, and giving thanks while still inside your circle will have a powerful impact on the outcome of any ritual your group has just performed while in your sacred space. To do this, have the group members sit on the floor (or ground) and close their eyes. Breathe deeply. Think of one thing you're grateful for and be willing to share it with the group. After a few moments, have the group leader signal that it's time for everyone to begin sharing their thoughts by softly ringing a bell. Simply go from person to person and allow each member to give thanks about one thing in their life. This gesture of giving thanks while in the magic circle will pay you back in positive ways many times over, because your expression of gratefulness as a group will be heard by the cosmos.

Merry Meet, Merry Part

If you can do only one farewell activity, let it be this one. "Merry meet, merry part" is usually used as a goodbye. It's one of the oldest Wiccan sayings. What it suggests is that coven members, even when apart, are still connected. It's a pleasant greeting but should only be used at Wiccan gatherings.

For this farewell activity I like to add a simple dance movement, since dancing is one of the most ancient forms of expression used in a magic circle. All members, including the leader, should stand and hold hands. Begin moving in the direction the leader says, which will probably be clockwise. Then chant or sing this rhyme:

> Hand to hand,
> Heart to heart.
> Merry meet,
> Merry part!

Move as quickly and dance as long as you want. This should be a joyful moment when all of you feel connected. If the leader wishes, the dance can be made more elaborate by moving in a spiral pattern.

· · · · · · · · · · · ·

Magic-circle activities serve to make members feel more comfortable with one another. They should help members feel that they're part of a caring community, but most importantly, they should be fun.

James Kambos *is a writer and folk artist. He writes for many Llewellyn annuals and enjoys studying numerous magical traditions. He writes from his home in Southern Ohio.*

Illustrator: Jennifer Hewitson

Creating Your Own
Coven Website

Elizabeth Barrette

In today's world, cyberspace provides a vital avenue of connection for most people. Members of a far-flung culture, such as Pagans, have an easier time finding each other through social networks, websites, and other routes. This creates a stronger, more cohesive Pagan community and allows us to find more people who are interested in exploring nature religions. So if you have a coven or other Pagan group, a website offers many advantages. It helps you keep track of members and events. It's a place to archive ritual scripts and other liturgy. It provides a safe method of contact for reaching new people. Let's take a look at how you can build a site for that.

Website Hosting

Your first choice involves hosting. Where will your site be on the Web? This affects how much it will cost, what kinds of programs and other tools you'll be using, and many other factors.

If you have plenty of computer skills, you can build your own website. Internet service providers often include hosting space for their clients. You can customize your site to do exactly what you need, whether you are building the site from scratch or using a modular buildware package like WordPress to assemble the pieces you want. This takes more time but delivers a more precise result. However, you also have to attract traffic from scratch, which can be done by joining webrings or other promotional groups. If you don't have the skills to design a site by yourself, you may be able to find or hire someone to help you.

For those of us who are not computer wizards, commercial website hosts offer a more user-friendly option. These include some blog hosts as well as places like Weebly. You sign up with them, they assign you some space, and you use their proprietary products to select the elements you want, such as the skin (colors and boxes in a template), illustrations, function tools (such as a search bar or donation button), and so forth. A good one will give you the chance to switch between a simple drag-and-drop menu or get into the code itself. It's harder to customize, especially if you want things they didn't plan for, but it's a lot easier to use. You may also get the advantage of traffic from other people in the same host network who make topical searches to find other people's pages.

Accessibility, Usability, and Aesthetics

Basic website design principles focus on accessibility, usability, and aesthetics. Accessibility determines how many people can see/hear what you have posted. Usability means how well your site works. Aesthetics means how the site looks.

Accessibility matters to your audience size. Some people have vision, hearing, mobility, or other limitations that make using some websites difficult or impossible. Never undercut your potential audience! You want as many people as possible to be able to use your website. So, for example, make sure the text is easy to read and has high contrast against the background, the images have text labels, and the site does not auto-play music. There are websites that not only describe how to make your site accessible but also allow you to key in your URL (Internet address) and a program will analyze how accessible it is and give recommendations for fixing any flaws.

Usability concerns how your website does its job. That means putting important things where people will see them and making the labels clear. Put the most vital content at the top and toward the left, where viewers start reading. Put less important things farther down or right. Choose clear, concise titles. Use divider bars, columns, and images to break up large blocks of text. Use cut tags or links to subpages so you can summarize basic ideas and then point people to more detailed explanations. Sort large categories (like sabbats) into smaller subcategories (like Samhain, Yule, etc.) so the main menu stays concise while the site still holds plenty of information.

Aesthetics make your site appealing. Here you're choosing colors, fonts, pictures, and other decorative elements. Don't go nuts making it look fancy; that just makes it harder to use. Pick high-contrast colors that are moderate enough to avoid eyestrain. Color changes tell people what is important, like when you put the text in black and the titles in green. Aim for fonts that have some visual interest but are still simple enough to read easily. Try to find photos, illustrations, and icons with large, clear shapes that will make sense even under imperfect circumstances. Select elements that match one another. If you are working from a host's template, much of this work is done for you. Just look for things to add that go well with it.

What to Include in Your Website

Website content is flexible. You can put pretty much anything you want on your site. So think about what your coven does and what you want people to know about it. Most covens want to post enough to help new people find them and keep current members organized—but not open the door to harassers. You may want to lock parts of your site with a password so only members can see them. Here are some things that many Pagans like to put on a coven website.

Bylaws or Charter

If you have any kind of description about your coven's goals and rules, post at least a summary of that. It tells people a lot about who you are, what you do, and whether they would be a good fit.

Calendar of Events

This helps current members plan ahead for your sabbats, esbats, classes, and other activities. It shows potential members what you're offering so they can think about what they'd like to attend. You should specify whether events are open to the public or for members only.

Covenstead

Most covens have one or more regular places of worship. Some are lucky enough to have a big house, yard, public building, or other facility. Start by describing that, including attractive features such as a pond, fire pit, or ritual room. If you're concerned about privacy, use close-up pictures of your altar layout and other objects (or stock images) instead of a long view of your house.

Main Page

This is the first thing people see on your site. Give your coven's name, your general goals and practices, and an overview of what folks can expect to find on your website. Remember, the vital content goes at the top left, then downward and rightward in descending order of importance.

Member List

Use descriptions and/or photos of your members to help people keep in touch with each other. You may list their magical interests, length of membership, contact information, and other details. Be careful: the more you include, the more trouble it can cause in the wrong hands. For this reason, member lists are often available only to other members.

RITUALS

Post text and photos from some of your most successful rituals. This helps members remember why they like your coven and shows potential members what they can expect if they start attending. Mix sabbats and esbats, indoors and outdoors, and small and large events if possible. Rituals encourage new people to join your coven so they can stand in circle with you.

SITE MAP AND MENU

These are essential navigational tools. The site map is a linked list of all the pages on your website. The menu is a bar of titles for your subpages and is usually located at the top, bottom, left side, or right side of the screen. Clicking on a title takes users to that page.

SPELLS

People search for spells all the time. Spells are great because people can do them at home. Along with rituals, this content helps attract visitors, who may stick around if they like your material.

Putting It Together

To create a website, first decide what you want to accomplish with it and write down some preliminary ideas. Choose a host for your site. Select or construct a template for making pages. Make the menu, putting it at the top or left side; try to use one-word titles for the tabs if possible. Add other navigation, social-networking, and infrastructure tools, such as search bars or contact boxes.

Fill in your main page. Make sure it contains all the most vital material, including a way to contact you. Use this space to summarize both your coven and the rest of your website. It needs to be catchy and informative so that people feel your site and coven are worth exploring further.

Next, make your subpages. Add text and images for each topic. Use a fractal pattern to organize them; that is, your main page leads to the subpages for your categories, and most of those categories have their own subpages. For example, Main Page: Events: Classes, Esbats, Sabbats.

Finally, add the finishing touches. Include details such as links to external websites, which help connect your site to the rest of the Web so people can find it and search engines will list it. Proofread to remove any mistakes. You really need another person to look over your draft, because they'll see things you missed. Polish it one last time.

Publish your new coven website. Promote it through whichever social networks or other venues your members frequent. You may also want to list it on The Witches' Voice or other Pagan hubs.

Resources

WEBSITE ACCESSIBILITY

www.w3.org/WAI/intro/accessibility.php

www.washington.edu/accessibility/web

www.powermapper.com/products/sortsite/checks/accessibility-checks

WEBSITE AESTHETICS

www.shire.net/learnwebdesign/aesthetics.htm

http://blog.teamtreehouse.com/3-simple-design-tests-to-improve
  -your-aesthetics

WEBSITE HOSTING

www.pcmag.com/article2/0,2817,2424725,00.asp

www.weebly.com

Website Usability

http://drpete.co/blog/25-point-website-usability-checklist

www.usability.gov

User Viewing Patterns

http://webdesign.tutsplus.com/articles/understanding-the-f-layout
  -in-web-design--webdesign-687

http://webdesign.tutsplus.com/articles/understanding-the-z-layout
  -in-web-design--webdesign-28

The Witches' Voice

www.witchvox.com

Elizabeth Barrette *has been involved with the Pagan community for more than twenty-five years. She served as managing editor of PanGaia for eight years and dean of studies at the Grey School of Wizardry for four years. Her book* Composing Magic: How to Create Magical Spells, Rituals, Blessings, Chants, and Prayers *explains how to combine writing and spirituality. She enjoys magical crafts, historical religions, and gardening for wildlife. Visit her blog,* The Wordsmith's Forge (*http://ysabetwordsmith.livejournal.com*)*, or her website,* PenUltimate Productions (*http://penultimateproductions.weebly.com*)*. Her coven site, with extensive Pagan materials, is* Greenhaven Tradition (*http://green haventradition.weebly.com*).

Illustrator: Kathleen Edwards

Under a Blood Moon: A Family Ritual

Monica Crosson

As October's Blood Moon rose over cragged peaks, pouring ethereal light upon the ever-moving water of the Sauk River, my family and I filed down a winding path lit by the flickering jack-o'-lanterns and canning-jar lanterns that hung from skeletal trees. Autumn's chill wrapped around us, and we shivered as we made our way to our altar tucked beneath the arms of a vine maple and decorated with mums, apples, walnuts, and pictures of loved ones who had passed on, to pay our respects.

Included among the photographs were pictures of my two Stellas, one my grandmother and the other my friend—two beautiful crones full of sage advice whom I'd had the honor to know. My grandmother had propagated my love of gardening and my friend had fertilized that love, allowing it to bloom. There were others, too: great aunts and uncles, friends whose time on Earth seemed much too short, and countless lost pets.

That year, among the old photos were three neatly crayoned portraits of my daughter Chloe's chickens—Lavender, Maisie, and Sunshine—and a picture of my son Elijah's cat, Salem. Ironically, as Chloe wiped away the salty reminder of her loss, she was petting the culprit in her chickens' demise—a golden lab named Yeti. "It's okay," she choked out. "I forgive you."

We lit candles for each and left a few sprigs of rosemary (for remembrance), then filed slowly to our family's circle on the edge of the Sauk River—a threshold between worlds—as my eldest son strummed out a haunting tune. The music faded and the circle was cast. We all played a role, which made the ritual feel more magickal somehow. The Blood Moon rose higher and the moonlight seemed to dance as it flooded our ritual space. A breeze seemed to pick up as the cone of power rose, and I remember a lump forming firmly in my throat. I truly felt the presence of the God and the Goddess, and I hoped they were pleased.

. . . .

Choosing to allow your children to be active in ritual can be a wonderful way to connect spiritually with them, help give them a solid spiritual base, foster deep bonds between family members, and provide structure and security. I do understand that there are many reasons practicing Pagans have for keeping their activities private and not involving their children. Some people live in an area where it might be dangerous for them to come out of the broom closet, so they feel they are protecting their children. There are others who feel they can't be open because they are the noncustodial parent and fear repercussions from the non-practicing custodial parent. Still others believe that children should be kept open-minded and be free to choose their own spiritual path.

Though my husband, Steve, and I definitely feel that there are many paths to deity and would be fine if our children chose to follow another spiritual path, we still thought it was important to at least lay those first bricks to a sound spiritual foundation. Our first and biggest lesson to our children growing up was the Wiccan Rede, "An it harm none, do as ye will," not just in our magickal practices but in our everyday lives as well. So it seemed a natural next step for us to involve our children in our practices.

When the children were young, instead have involving them in a circle, we sang to the moon and made fairy houses and blew horns at dawn at Yule to welcome the newborn sun. We made crafts and wrote plays and spent every second we could in the best temple there is: *nature*. As the children grew older, we began with simple rituals full of song and dance. When casting a circle, we used simple rhymes that were easy to remember and packed a much bigger punch for the little ones. By the time they were seven or eight, they seemed to have a pretty firm grasp on what it meant to be Pagan, and as teenagers, they could plan and write rituals on their own.

Ritual with Children

Here are some simple ways to make ritual with your children a fun and magickal experience.

INCORPORATE LOTS OF SINGING AND MOVEMENT

Kids love songs and movement, be it dancing, drumming, singing, or ringing bells. Shake, baby, shake!

CREATE SACRED SPACE IN A FUN AND SIMPLE MANNER

Casting your circle with simple rhymes makes it fun for younger children and helps to impart simple lessons about circle casting, the elements, ritual tools, and so forth.

GIVE YOUR CHILDREN JOBS

Empower your magickal little ones by giving them a sense of responsibility. Give them a role to play, whether it's speaking a line or lighting a candle. The more active they are in ritual, the better they will understand the sacredness of the event.

Keep Magick Simple

Don't involve your children in spells that are not age-appropriate or that they have little or no understanding of.

Incorporate Seasonal Crafts

If you have children who love to express themselves artistically, arts and crafts are a fun way to instill spiritual lessons and get them involved with sabbat preparation. My children were big into making masks and acting out plays that they would write to coincide with our sabbat celebrations. If you need ideas for artsy projects, Pinterest is a wonderful site for craft ideas (warning: it's addictive!).

Involve Older Children in Planning

As the kids get older, empower them by having them plan a ritual. You might be surprised at what they come up with. When she was fifteen, my daughter, Chloe, and her friend Hannah planned our Midsummer ritual, and it was absolutely wonderful! It's a real confidence booster for the kids, and as busy adults, it's nice to have the extra help.

Serve Kid-Friendly Cakes and Ale

Remember to keep the cakes and ale kid-friendly. Cookies and juice or hot cocoa are nice alternatives. Better yet, turn your little ones into Kitchen Witches by letting them help choose and prepare the cakes and ale.

Keep Ritual Short

Smaller children have short attention spans. A ritual for a preschooler might include singing and dancing under the full moon, followed by a cookie and some hot cocoa. Speak at your child's level. Nothing bores children more than having to stand still while someone recites pages and pages of script. Let ritual grow as they do.

Keep the Ritual Area Safe

Before involving kids in ritual, make sure all candles are secure in proper candleholders. If performing ritual outdoors, pick up any sticks, rocks, or debris that may be a tripping hazard. Any fire should be built in a fire pit or cauldron and kept small.

Hold Separate Rituals for Adults and Children

Especially when your kids are small, it's sometimes easier to have separate rituals—one geared toward the kids and one for the adults. As families grew within my coven, we did just that. As near as possible to the sabbat celebration, we planned events for our kids. On the evening of the sabbat, it was just adults.

Don't muffle children's natural magickal abilities because they interfere with the script. In fact, when it comes to kids, you might want to throw out the script. Your script may say one thing, but if just dancing is working for the kids, just dance. Choose a simple outline for your ritual and always be prepared for the unexpected. Go with the flow.

A Moon of Many Names

Every family ritual is important to me, but there is something about our Blood Moon ritual that seems particularly poignant, and it has become my favorite. October's full moon is known by many names. The days are becoming shorter, and as the leaves fade, the veil becomes thin as we pass into the dark half of the year. This was the time of the hunt for ancient (and some modern) people, so October's full moon is sometimes called the Hunter's Moon. To some, when the full moon in October falls closer to the autumn equinox, it is called the Harvest Moon. To others it was known as the Blood Moon, for it was also a time of butchering domestic animals Although my family celebrates the Blood Moon, it really has nothing to do with butchering livestock. It has deeper connotations for us, roots that reach far into the soil and spread across North America and into Ireland, England, Germany, and Scandinavia. Blood for us means "family."

I bet I know what you're thinking: "Yeah, duh, Monica. That's what October's Samhain is all about: our ancestors." But as parents of young children, we realized quickly that we couldn't juggle the sacredness of a Samhain ritual and the excitement of trick-or-treating and Halloween parties for the kids all in one evening. Our solution: a Samhain-like ritual just for our family on the night of October's Blood Moon. We used it not only to venerate our ancestors but also to celebrate our nuclear family. That way, on the night of Samhain, after an evening of haunting the town with our family, I was free to spend much-needed adult time with my coven at our Samhain ritual while Steve stayed home and put our little goblins to bed.

If you're interested in performing a Blood Moon ritual with your family, here is an example that includes a fun craft idea and some recipes. You will need to begin this craft a few days before the ritual. Older kids could do this by themselves, but younger ones will need assistance from a parent or older sibling.

Remembrance Besom

You will need:

- An interesting stick (found on the ground and not taken from a tree) or a dowel 3 to 4 inches long and about 1 inch in diameter to use as a handle

- Straw or other herb stalks

- Twine

- Rosemary twigs (for remembrance)

- Sage (for wisdom of the crone)

- Scissors

- Charms (such as moons, stars, skulls, etc.)

Soak the straw or herb stalks overnight in lukewarm water. When ready to make your besom, pat dry the straw. Place your stick or dowel on a table, and line straw along the handle approximately three inches from the bottom. Bind tightly with twine. Gently bend the stalks over the binding. Before securing, lay a few pieces of rosemary and sage onto the straw. Wrap with a couple inches of twine to secure. Let dry for a couple days. Decorate the handle by drawing or painting symbols of your choice. String a couple charms on twine and tie around the base of the broom. Before your Blood Moon ritual, let the kids use their new besoms to sweep away negativity from the circle.

Samhain Cider

   1 orange

   2 quarts apple cider

   3 cinnamon sticks

   ¼ cup brown sugar

   ½ teaspoon vanilla

   1 apple, sliced, with the slices studded with cloves

   Maraschino cherries

Slice the orange and place half in a large pan (or a slow cooker—this just takes much longer).

Add the apple cider, cinnamon sticks, brown sugar, vanilla, and apple slices studded with cloves. Warm the mixture (do not boil) for about half an hour. Remove the oranges, cinnamon sticks, and cloves. Place a slice of reserved orange, a few cherries, and a fresh cinnamon stick in large mugs and fill with the hot cider.

Soul Cakes

   ½ cup butter

   ½ cup baker's sugar

   3 egg yolks

   2 cups flour

   Cinnamon to taste

   ½ teaspoon vanilla

   ¼ cup raisins

   Milk

Cream butter and sugar in a bowl. Beat in egg yolks. Sift the flour and cinnamon into the butter mixture. Add the vanilla. Stir in the raisins and enough milk to make the dough soft. Shape the dough by hand into flat, round cakes about the size of a biscuit and place them on a greased cookie sheet. With the point of a sharp knife, cut a spiral circle into the tops of the cakes. Bake at 350°F for about ten to fifteen minutes or until brown.

Blood Moon/Samhain Ritual

Kids love to dress up, so before the ritual, let the kids go crazy with facepaint and costumes. Paint symbols in black, orange, and red on their faces and hands. Have them dress as fairies or in one-of-a-kind cloaks that they helped decorate.

Next, bring on the besoms. While the kids sweep away all negativity from your sacred space, beat the drums or sing fun songs.

Set up your altar with traditional Samhain decorations, which may include apples (for the divine), hazelnuts (wisdom), rosemary (remembrance), and sage (wisdom of the crone). Also have photographs and drawings of those you would like to remember and tealight candles for each.

Cast your circle in your own way. Then have one parent say the following:

The end of summer is upon us, and as we face the darkness, let us remember, we do not do it alone. For the veil is thin this night and the love of those who have crossed over shines upon us. Because we remember, they live on.

Then one by one have each family member go to the altar and light a tealight for the family member (or pet) they would like to remember. Have them pick up the photograph and share a story or fun memory of their loved one.

When you are done, close the circle in your own way.

Enjoy traditional soul cakes and hot apple cider for your cakes and ale. While doing so, play a few divination games or tell some good old-fashioned ghost stories.

. . . .

This year we will celebrate yet another Blood Moon. We will file down that same winding path we have followed for almost two decades. The trees that rattle their skeletal branches in the cool autumn breeze are a little taller and the salmonberry and Indian plum have become overgrown, but the power that is raised by us, the Crosson Witches, is strong. For we are a family bonded by blood and secure in the knowledge that we will always have each other. We will always have memories of those nights under a full Blood Moon. Thank Goddess for family!

Monica Crosson *is a Master Gardener who lives in the beautiful Pacific Northwest, happily digging in the dirt and tending her raspberries with her husband, three kids, two goats, two dogs, three cats, a dozen chickens, and Rosetta the donkey. She has been a practicing Witch for twenty years and is a member of Blue Moon Coven. Monica writes fiction for young adults and is the author of* Summer Sage.

Illustrator: Tim Foley

The Place of Thoughts and Emotions in Witchcraft

Raven Digitalis

Our thoughts and emotions make us who we are. I'm happy to say that the majority of Witches and magickal practitioners I've met are deep-thinking, emotionally sensitive individuals. That's a fact I'm very grateful for, because we all have such uniquely important roles to play in the world. Regardless of how we discovered the Craft, we find our hearts beating to the rhythm of nature. We also find that the natural world is reflected within us, through the cycles and stages of development of our bodies and minds. Like our plant and animal comrades, we are extensions of the natural world. Yet unlike plants and other animals, our thoughts and emotions tend to be particularly complex. Nonhuman animals exhibit emotions, of course, but what sets us humans apart is our level of attachment to our experiences. We emotionally and cognitively process things somewhat differently than other animals—there's no denying it! While we do indeed function like other animals in terms of biological instincts and basic emotions, we humans are a distinctly complex species of overthinkers and overfeelers.

I think it's safe for me to assume that you, dear reader, have a decent understanding of what thoughts and emotions are. Because thoughts and emotions are experiential, rattling off descriptions here and now would not do the subjects justice. In fact, numerous philosophers and theorists catalog the spectrums of human emotion and cognition in a multitude of ways—sometimes *vastly* different ways! However we choose to define them, our thoughts and emotions require recognition, responsibility, and awareness. If we own our thoughts and emotions, we own our magick.

Spellcasting, meditation, and prayer operate on both interior and exterior levels. Intentional focus in these scenarios, and indeed in life itself, resonates both cosmically (esoterically) and psychologically (mentally). The famed Hermetic axiom "As above, so below" may also be applied to the saying "As within, so without." Because of this connection with the micro (self) and the macro (universe), the ways in which we conduct our thoughts and emotional responses have an effect both on our personal perspective and on the global spiritual landscape. Thoughts, we find, are often directly linked to our emotional responses. For this reason, a magickal practitioner has a unique responsibility to exercise emotional awareness and mental precision, whether in daily life or in formal ritualistic endeavors.

Emotional Awareness

We humans, witchy or otherwise, are creatures of feeling. Emotions enrich our experience of life, deeply influencing our daily modes of thought and, for us, our regular magickal work. Aside from individuals who may suffer from a medical condition that directly relates to affective functioning, the great majority of individuals have access to the full, beautiful spectrum of human emotions. It's simply a matter of what we are tapped into at any given moment.

Everyone is psychologically wired differently from birth and from experience (and undoubtedly from those of previous lifetimes), which is why no emotional issue ever has a single solution or remedy. Everyone connects with emotions in a different manner. Emotions and emotional responses are a personal thing. Everyone has different emotional strengths and hindrances.

Emotions are fragile, it's true, but we are powerful beings. As dedicated magickal folk, we must strive to be honest with ourselves as much as we possibly can. This includes emotional honesty. No one can be expected to function at 100 percent self-awareness 24/7, but if we can keep our emotional tides in check on a regular basis, we soon find that life's ups, downs, twists, and turns don't have to overtake us every time.

Witches regularly practice "seeing through the veil," which also ideally applies to our *own* veil! The mind can play tricks at times. Emotions can feel all-pervasive if we don't take a step back and become an observer. This is why Buddhism and other Eastern spiritual paths stress the concepts of mindfulness and present-moment awareness. They've got a point!

Positive Thinking

While it might be easier said than done sometimes, positive thinking really is a key to our survival—not to mention our magickal success. If we can train our minds to default to optimism rather than pessimism, we find that the world is a beautiful place despite its dreadful challenges.

Choosing to think positively doesn't mean that we should put on happy masks or pretend that we're fine even when we're not. We can acknowledge our own troubles and simultaneously choose to shift our mental focus to a lighter and less somber state of perception.

Mindful redirection requires *humility*, one of the most valuable spiritual assets in the world. By remaining humble, we can easily learn from our mistakes and exercise forgiveness for ourselves and others. Through humility we can gracefully step back from our mental and emotional bodies so that we can redirect ourselves in a more spiritually and magickally conscious manner—and we can encourage others to do the same.

It takes practice to incorporate positive thinking into our daily routine. We need to exercise consistent self-awareness so we can make the spiritual choice to reroute our mind's reactions as necessary. Maintaining good humor and lightheartedness even at the worst of times can go a long way in helping ourselves and others.

Just like pessimism, optimism is contagious. As Witches and magickal practitioners, it's our duty to be constantly aware of our effect on the world and the people with whom we interact. The more we work on our own thoughts and modes of communication, the more we can help turn the world in a positive direction, bit by bit, moment by moment—and that's some *very* powerful magickal work.

Magick: Follow Your Thoughts

When people first find themselves attracted to Witchcraft and magickal spirituality, a great many of them are allured by the sense of power that can be gained from the "practical" applications of the magickal arts. I know I sure was! Eventually, this perspective tends to shift to a focus on empowerment rather than power or control. Increasing self-control and self-awareness is a million times more spiritually relevant than "doing magick" to get something. But still, sitting down and performing a spell to change one's own reality has its time and place.

In a sense, spellcasting occurs every day. Everyone actively co-creates reality whether they realize it or not. Spells, prayers, and intentional magick are not limited to occult ritual. Ritualistic procedures can be fulfilling, potent, and transformational, but I strongly argue that the most important ritual we perform is our day-to-day experience. For this reason, we must follow our thoughts.

Because thought is linked with intention, we find that magickal energy follows the flow of our thoughts. Thinking about something invokes its presence on some level; it's simply a matter of what we *do* with those thoughts. As a general rule, fearful thoughts attract a fearful experience, and loving thoughts attract a loving experience. In many ways, we magickal folk get to choose our experiences by intentionally directing our subtle energies on a daily basis.

Magick's Cognitive and Emotional Influences

Because our daily thoughts and actions are directly linked to our emotional responses, having an acute awareness of our emotional reactions will allow us to trace our thought patterns and distinguish illusion from objective understanding. Our thoughts influence our emotions and our emotions influence our thoughts. In an effort to gain emotional awareness, we can begin by actively choosing to focus on how we think. An easy way to do this is to regularly take a step back and consider how we perceive life, including ourselves, in any given moment. It's also worth considering that spellcraft is greatly accomplished by way of emotional energy. We are much more able to influence reality through intentional emotional projection than we are from simply "thinking" a spell or going through the motions without the emotions. Drinking a single drop of rosemary tea with the emotional intention of healing and protection is significantly more effective than drinking a whole gallon of the stuff without any emotional focus behind it.

Have you ever heard that old saying "Cast a spell and then forget about it"? It seems clear enough: weave your magick into the universe and then stop feeding it mental energy. The reasoning behind this idea is simple: if you forget about your magick, you leave it in the hands of the gods and spirits. In theory, this ensures that the magician won't agitate or nitpick the energy that has already been projected; it's been put out there and doesn't need to be influenced any further. The mere idea of "forgetting" about a spell implies that a person's everyday thoughts have an effect on the already cast spell. I believe that most practitioners would agree with this perspective. But at the same time, does "forgetting" about a spell really work as well in practice?

A Witch's thoughts and emotions can either reinforce or unravel their magick. That's a huge thing! We can be our own best magickal cheerleader or our own worst enemy. As our thoughts and emotions interplay in our daily lives, we can choose to have them reinforce our magickal work or have them undo it. Truly, this is not something to be taken lightly. If we actively channel our daily thoughts and emotions concerning our magick, we can add a boost of daily power to spells and rituals that have been performed. This is why we see things like seven-day candles in Santería and similar traditions. Daily reinforcement goes a long way. If we want to empower our magickal work, we need to channel our thoughts and emotions as they arise, whether they are attached to our current magickal work or not. As many readers are aware, magick is not about *doing*; it is about *being*.

Mental and Emotional Overload

Life is tricky. It's easy to become emotionally overwhelmed to the point of hopelessness, but many of the tormenting thoughts that inspire these emotional states are illusory. It can be challenging to work ourselves out of emotional overload, especially if it has become a routine activity, but where there's a will, there's a way. Sometimes this means making lifestyle modifications and working more diligently with techniques of self-awareness. The following are a few options to consider on your own journey to cognitive and emotional well-being.

Counseling

I believe that *everyone* deserves counseling and therapy from time to time. When life is just too overwhelming, individuals who are professionally trained in the workings of the mind can be of great assistance. There are many different styles of counseling, therapy, and life coaching to choose from. Many professionals have online biographies that can help seekers get a better idea of their counseling style, specialties, and per-

sonal values. (Please also note that free or discount therapists are available in most cities.)

JOURNALING AND ART

Possibly one of the most underrated psychological activities, keeping a journal or diary can greatly assist in getting thoughts and emotions "out there." By expressing our thoughts and emotions in a private manner, the energy becomes externalized so it doesn't have to run amok in our head. Similarly, artistic expression of any type serves to creatively channel our innermost thoughts and emotions. Both journaling and art can also be transformational acts of magickal intention.

MEDICINE

I should note that none of the advice herein is a substitute for medical advice. For many emotionally sensitive individuals, a combination of medication and lifestyle changes can produce dramatic healing effects. This category of "medicine" is not limited to Western pharmaceuticals; many people find naturopathic and herbal medicine to be extremely effective. Everybody has a different constitution, so there is no "right" medicinal answer for everyone. If you feel that this option might benefit you, I encourage you to speak with a physician and other healthcare professionals to determine if medicine would aid in your own mental and emotional balance.

Mindfulness

A term frequently used in both Buddhism and psychological circles, *mindfulness* implies self-awareness. To become mindful is to take a step back from our thoughts and emotions in order to gain greater psychological equilibrium; in this way, we can take a moment to *detach* from our mind and emotions without actually *disconnecting*. Mindfulness encompasses the idea of present-moment awareness: to focus on the events of the now rather than stress out about the past or the future. If we can train ourselves to observe our thoughts and emotions as frequently as possible, we can more easily detach at any given moment. We are not our thoughts. We are not our emotions. These are components that help create this thing we call "self," and with the aid of daily mindfulness, we can take a step back and choose to be the one in control.

Ritual

Who doesn't love a good ritual? Solid ceremonial standards like the Lesser Banishing Ritual of the Pentagram can balance our cognitive and emotional bodies while simultaneously invoking the spiritual realm. Even a powerful recitation of the Witches' Rune, the Wiccan Rede, or another magically poetic text can have instant calming effects. If you are creating your own ceremony, consider incorporating visualizations focused on dumping excessive energy into the earth. Similarly, it's wise to practice grounding by performing visualizations such as tree rooting. For those who are especially emotionally sensitive, you may wish to perform a self-made ritual or spell in the bathtub or shower or in a body of water.

Sleep, Diet, and Exercise

One cannot underestimate the power of a good night's sleep, regular exercise, and a healthy diet. Our bodies are the divine temples in which our spirits have the pleasure of incarnating at this moment in time; taking care of our bodies is tending to our souls. It may take time to discover your unique needs and preferences in all of these realms, but the mind and emotions can greatly shift toward the positive once a personal balance is realized and diligently maintained.

Yoga and Meditation

Yoga and meditation have profound benefits psychologically, emotionally, physically, and spiritually. There are numerous styles, schools, and philosophies of both yoga and meditation; many would say that the two practices are inextricably linked. Integrating any measure of these practices on a regular basis can help balance any spiritual seeker emotionally and mentally. While yoga and meditation can seem intimidating to newcomers, they are much easier to practice than is commonly believed. In many ways, these practices are inherently wired into our brains and bodies; it's just a matter of learning the techniques. It's no wonder that the various styles of yoga and meditation have been practiced since time immemorial and will most certainly continue to be practiced.

Sources

Aron, Elaine N. *The Highly Sensitive Person: How to Thrive When the World Overwhelms You.* Secaucus, NJ: Birch Lane Press, 1996.

Bennett-Goleman, Tara. *Emotional Alchemy: How the Mind Can Heal the Heart.* New York: Harmony Books, 2001.

Digitalis, Raven. *Esoteric Empathy: A Magickal & Metaphysical Guide to Emotional Sensitivity.* Woodbury, MN: Llewellyn, 2016.

Farrar, Janet, and Stewart Farrar. A *Witches' Bible: The Complete Witches' Handbook*. Custer, WA: Phoenix Publishing, 1981.

Goleman, Daniel. *Emotional Intelligence: Why It Can Matter More Than IQ*. New York: Bantam Books, 1995.

Lewis, Michael, Jeannette M. Haviland-Jones, and Lisa Feldman Barrette, eds. 2nd edition. *Handbook of Emotions*. New York: Guilford Press, 2004.

McLaren, Karla. *The Art of Empathy: A Complete Guide to Life's Most Essential Skill*. Boulder, CO: Sounds True, 2013.

Mesich, Kyra, PsyD. *The Sensitive Person's Survival Guide: An Alternative Health Answer to Emotional Sensitivity and Depression*. Lincoln, NE: iUniverse, 2000.

Raven Digitalis (*Missoula, MT*) *is the author of* Esoteric Empathy, Shadow Magick Compendium, Planetary Spells & Rituals, *and* Goth Craft. *He is a Neopagan Priest and cofounder of an Eastern Hellenistic nonprofit community temple called Opus Aima Obscuræ (OAO). Also trained in Eastern philosophies and Georgian Witchcraft, Raven has been an earth-based practitioner since 1999, a Priest since 2003, a Freemason since 2012, and an empath all his life. He holds a degree in anthropology from the University of Montana and is also a professional tarot reader, DJ, small-scale farmer, and animal rights advocate. Contact him at www.ravendigitalis.com, www.facebook.com/ravendigitalis, www.opusaimaobscurae.org, and www .facebook.com/opusaimaobscurae.*

Illustrator: Rik Olson

Seasonal Frustration: How to Celebrate the Sabbats When the Weather Is Challenging

Michael Furie

One of the cornerstones of most Pagan practice is a reverence for nature and the physical and spiritual forces behind natural phenomena. This reverence is one reason the solar festivals are celebrated. This being the case, it would seem that no matter what the season, the weather conditions would be welcomed and enjoyed, but this isn't always true. Frankly, the weather is just awful sometimes. It can be difficult to plan a beautiful Yuletide sabbat celebration when everyone is snowed in and the wind chill factor takes the temperature into the below-zero range.

Similarly, it is nearly impossible (and rather unsafe) to have a wonderful Lughnasadh holiday complete with bonfire and outdoor games if the weather is oppressively hot and your local area is suffering from a severe drought.

Though it may be tempting to grumble and complain (and I do) or even to give up entirely (which I refuse to do), it is much more productive and in keeping with our witchy forebears to modify our plans and adjust to the prevailing conditions. Just because we may revere nature, we needn't feel obligated to automatically enjoy whatever forces surround us or feel guilty if we dislike the weather of a particular season. As Witches and Pagans, it is incumbent upon us to live from our authentic self, and as such, if we can't stand a ton of snow or extreme heat, we needn't feel inadequate. The questions then become, (1) If I don't care for the weather of a particular season, should I even celebrate it? and (2) If I do celebrate it, how should I do so?

Personally, I think it is important to mark each holiday in some way. It keeps us in tune with the rhythm of nature, and also it just feels like the right thing to do, even if there are some difficulties. The key to celebrating even in harsh conditions is modification. Most books and websites that describe Pagan religions have some type of general narrative regarding the progression of the holidays and how they link together, from the dark hibernation time through birth, growth, and harvest and back down to

I think it is important to mark each holiday in some way. It keeps us in tune with the rhythm of nature, and also it just feels like the right thing to do, even if there are some difficulties. The key to celebrating even in harsh conditions is modification.

the hibernation of winter. Aside from the basic predominant themes of the holidays, there exist underlying and alternative aspects to the sabbats that provide us with things to focus on other than the shifting weather patterns of the time. Since the primary weather-based challenges of holiday celebrations can be broken down into two basic categories—too hot or too cold—I will cover the days as divided anciently, the sabbats of the dark half of the year and the sabbats of the light half, respectively. Though we were all taught that the earth experiences four seasons, in many regions there really are just two: hot and cold. Let us look at the fall/wintertime sabbats first, as many people feel unhappy during extended periods of cold weather.

In many places, by the time Samhain/Halloween rolls around, the cold weather has already set in for the season. Many children have had to suffer through a cold, rainy Halloween. Even though the main theme of Samhain usually relates to darkness, cold, spirits, death, and the Otherworld, it is also considered the beginning of the new year. One practice for Samhain is to harness the energy of the day and channel it into a projection, a sort of New Year's resolution/wish spell. This can be enacted through choice of costume and decoration for the day. Solar and warm colors can be worn, fires can be lit, and hot, hearty foods (soups, stews, etc.) can be served, all with the goal of encouraging warmth in our lives. Now, I am not suggesting that you perform active weather magic to effect an external change, but rather that you set the magical intention for yourself to continue to draw warmth throughout the cold time of year. Practically speaking, this magic can result in various forms of experience, such as travel to warmer locations, increased time at home out of the weather, an inner strength that seems to ward off feeling cold, and many other possibilities. There is no real rule that says Samhain has to be cold, dark, and spooky. The acknowledgment, reverence, and celebration are the most important aspects; the individual forms and methods used are simply the blessing of personal practice.

In places where Samhain has already brought in an icy chill, by the time the winter solstice arrives, the short days, long nights, seemingly endless snowstorms, and bitter winds can have even the most enthusiastic Witch tired of the cold and ready for spring. Luckily, the energy and power of this particular sabbat is attuned to just that type of mindset. Though this solstice is the onset of the season of winter, it is also the beginning of growth in the solar cycle and is considered the sun's rebirth. This works out perfectly if our desire is to rid ourselves of the cold. If the streets are clear and the electricity and heater are working, then it's relatively easy to plan an enjoyable holiday that focuses on family and warmth. But if the weather is uncooperative and/or the power goes out, then the whole day can feel cold and lonely. To overcome this, it is a good idea to work traditional sympathetic magic to encourage the rebirth of the sun. In many (if not all) Pagan traditions, it is customary to light fires to encourage the sun's growth. Whether it be a candle, a fire kindled in a cauldron, a yule log in a fireplace, or some combination of methods, the purpose is to beckon forth the powers of the sun. According to ancient thought, Witches and Pagans needed to conduct the sabbat rites in order to maintain the natural balance, with the belief that if they didn't, then the sun, moon, and earth wouldn't have enough power to continue the cycle.

For me, this notion parallels the modern scientific concept known as the "observer effect," wherein the person conducting an experiment, simply through the act of observation, cannot help but affect the outcome. Whether necessary or not, the magical act of energizing the sun does create a type of cooperative bond, a joining of the Witch's intent with that of the solar energy. This psychic link, once established (and reinforced over the years), can really strengthen a person's ability to draw upon the energy and heat of the sun. I should

make it clear that this isn't weather magic; rather, it is a participatory action of acknowledgment and celebration of the solar cycle and a reaching out energetically to unite with the shift taking place. This work doesn't have the same potential for mishap since it's not about manifestation but instead is focused on connection. Said connection can then be used to draw in the feeling of warmth to help overcome some of the cold. At this time of year, meditating on the heat and power of the sun (essentially a drawing down of the sun's energy) and feeling it pouring onto you to foster energy and warmth is a valuable exercise and can be done as often as needed throughout the season.

Though the holiday of Imbolc is said to be when the first stirrings of spring occur, in many places the only thing that has sprouted is yet another flurry of snow and cold weather. For me, the antidote to the cold is through a somewhat underrated part of this sabbat: food. Seeds, spicy foods, dairy, and lamb are traditional foods for this day, but I like to bake breads since nothing can warm up a home faster than using the oven. Even if baking is not your strong suit, there are many baking mixes that can be repurposed for magical use. If the mix is more of a batter, such as for cornbread, magical symbols can be traced into the butter or oil on the pan before the batter is poured so the bread will absorb the intention as it bakes. For firmer dough, runes and symbols such as a sun disc can be cut into it before baking. A nice, warm dinner party can be the central focus for a very enjoyable Imbolc.

At the Spring Equinox sabbat, the weather has usually started to warm up, but now a new problem can rear its ugly head: allergies. This particular problem has plagued me for most of my life, so spring isn't exactly my favorite time of year. I'm very grateful to live in an age in which we have access to antihistamines, but it is still almost impossible for me to be outdoors for any length of time without sneezing, wheezing, and itching. For those of us with allergies, outdoor celebrations aren't the best choice. A nice indoor option, especially in colder climates, is to plant seeds for herbs that are aligned with a magical goal (spring is an excellent time for initiating long-term magic), charging the seeds with intent, and caring for them as they grow throughout the season in order to manifest your goals. This becomes a physical manifestation of the power of the equinox. Though dull and not very celebratory, spring cleaning (both physical and magical) is also a good and practical way of tuning in to the energy of the Spring Equinox. A house blessing afterward can bring the magic of the day back into the home and enliven the holiday.

The light half of the year officially begins on May 1st and includes Beltane, Midsummer, Lughnasadh, and the Autumn Equinox. These holidays, being the equal but opposite counterparts of the winter sabbats, can present the equal but opposite problem of being way too hot. The light half of the year begins with Beltane, the sabbat of life and fertility. It is exactly opposite Samhain on the Wheel of the Year and so is one of the most powerful sabbats. Whether this day will be on the hot side or still cold depends on the region. Either way, a simple means of harnessing the energy of the day is to leave a bowl of water outdoors (perhaps with herbs such as meadowsweet or basil soaking in it) overnight on May Eve and let it soak up the May morning sun. This infuses it with the power of the day, making it a sabbat holy water. This water can be used for blessings, hex breaking, and general anointing purposes.

Midsummer, the actual summer solstice, follows Beltane and can be quite warm. Where I live, the temperature has almost invariably climbed into the 100-degree range by this point, so holding an indoor celebration or (ironically) waiting until nighttime to have an outdoor ritual are usually the best choices. Even though most people focus on the solar/fire aspects of the day, Midsummer has a secondary theme of well and water magic. Much like the duality of the winter solstice, the

 summer sabbat marks the peak of solar power and is the longest day of the year but it also means that from this point on the days will get shorter until winter. Sympathetic magic to balance the heat with coolness can consist of floating a candle in a water-filled cauldron and letting it burn until it is consumed by the water, or burning a candle in an empty vessel and then dousing it with a cup of water as a ritual act.

The hottest sabbat is usually Lughnasadh, on August 1st. Last year, the weather was so hot where I live that the taper candle on my kitchen table actually melted and bent like a cane. Needless to say, with the weather that hot, I wasn't about to celebrate outdoors. Since the candles were melting without even being lit, I decided to use some electric candles. Electricity and fire are related, so even though the candles are artificial, they do set the appropriate atmosphere. Aside from the harvest and grain themes of Lughnasadh, a custom of the day is to cool the heat of the sun to ensure that the crops will endure long enough to be fully harvested. If there is a ritual fire or an actual candle, dousing it with water can be the ritual act for cooling the sun. If not, another option is to water a garden, if you have one, using the water to protect the plants from the August heat.

The Autumn Equinox sabbat is a bit tricky. In some areas it is still hot out and hardly feels like fall, but in other areas the cold has already set in and it feels more like winter. In either case, since this sabbat is considered the Witches' Thanksgiving, a good way to celebrate is to make a nice dinner from harvest vegetables and grains. Most of the traditional Thanksgiving foods fit the criteria. The most important aspect of the day is, after all, thankfulness.

· · · · · · · · · · · ·

There is more than one way to observe a sabbat. Marking the day needn't be about slavishly adhering to methods and procedures that may not resonate with our own experience. Since the sabbats are about connecting to the earth, it is actually better to adjust to the local atmosphere rather than conform to a set pattern made centuries ago for areas thousands of miles away. This keeps the sabbats relevant to our present lives. The holidays aren't always about formal ritual or involved energy work. If the weather or season is not conducive to heavy ceremony, the day can still be celebrated, honored, and, most importantly, enjoyed as part of the Wheel of the Year.

Michael Furie *is the author of* Spellcasting: Beyond the Basics, Supermarket Magic, *and more, and has been a practicing Witch for more than twenty years. An American Witch, he practices in the Irish tradition and is a priest of the Cailleach. Michael lives in Northern California and can be found online at www.michaelfurie.com.*

Illustrator: Bri Hermanson

Working with the Dark Moon

Lisa Mc Sherry

When I first started on the path of Witchcraft, I was told that no White Witch would ever work a spell at the dark of the moon. I was told that time was reserved for those who walk the left-hand path, casting manipulative spells and using sinister forces to work their will on others.

If you think I just used a lot of loaded language, you would be correct. What I came to learn through following my own intuition, with a few helpful guides, was that the moon's other face can be powerful and transformative, which can feel very scary. What I was told wasn't wrong; it was just steeped in superstition and fear.

The dark moon is the time when, astronomically speaking, the moon lies between the earth and sun and is completely in shadow, receiving no light from the sun, and therefore is not visible to the naked eye. (On most calendars this is called the new moon, but that time does not truly occur until a few days later when a thin sliver of moon is visible once again.) The dark moon happens at the time opposite the full moon, easily seen on any calendar that shows the waxing and waning lunar cycle. Do not confuse this with the moon void of course, which is truly a bad time for spellwork (because there isn't any lunar energy to work with). Women may follow the lunar cycle with their menstrual cycle, ovulating and at the height of fertility at the full moon, then shedding blood at the dark moon. For every woman, menstruation is always a good time to withdraw and go within, to look upon her darker self with soft eyes and a warm heart.

The dark moon is a doorway to the underworld. This is a good time to work with the crossroads and ancestors, as well as any deities associated with the dark and the underworld. The Graces (or Fates), Hecate, the Morrighan, Cerridwen, Osiris, and Ereshkigal are all good

examples, and there seem to be more goddesses than gods; perhaps this is a legacy of the polarity between the dark/lunar/feminine and the light/solar/masculine. I work with Mercury in his aspect of psychopomp, traveler between the underworld and our realm. Most deities have a dark side you can work with, so although you may want to choose new ones for specific work, it is rarely necessary to find new gods or goddesses.

The gift of the dark moon is that of soul-searching. It is a time to listen, integrate, and set intentions that will bring you into harmony with yourself during the waxing moon. My coven and I have worked with the dark moon as part of our annual cycle of rituals for more than thirteen years now, and I believe the dark moon rituals are the most transformative ones we hold. We believe there must be balance in Witchcraft: within/without, light/dark, male/female, and so on. We don't just do sabbats, but also esbats; and if we do full moon rituals, we must do dark moon rituals as well. So we created a specific cycle of rituals, done during the winter, starting with the first dark moon after Samhain. In that ritual we meet the dark goddess in her aspect as crone and we are reborn from her cauldron. Over the following four lunations we use guided meditation within a ritual framework to go within and explore aspects of our shadow self, always with a guide and always with time to explore the meaning of what we have learned. These ritual explorations take place within a circle cast widdershins, which gives us the opportunity to explore how the energy feels compared to deosil. Our emphasis is on looking within and listening to what deity tells us, what we need to know at this time and in this place.

The dark moon is a glorious time for spellwork involving cursing (yes, I said it) and curse-breaking, unraveling previous spells, unbinding, and banishing. It is an excellent time to work spells to break addictions. One example would be to create sacred space and then force all of your negative thoughts and energy regarding your addiction into an egg. Then cry and bathe the egg in your tears; scream and let the sound cover the shell completely. Take a magic marker and write all over the egg. Color it black, still pouring all of your addiction out of you and into the egg. When you are done, wrap the egg in a paper towel and then in a paper bag. Carefully take it to a crossroads and throw it as hard as you can into the center. Immediately turn and walk away. Do not look back.

My personal preference is to use the dark moon to work with the shadow self and to find balance. Part of the power of the dark moon is to break down old systems and let go, along with a doing a review of how we've been living and what we believe. We then can plant new seeds and watch them manifest at the full moon (or later in the year). The phrase I use is "I set the intention in the dark of the moon to…" This is a time to look at which things about ourselves we might banish (habits, perhaps?), making room for new things to embrace and integrate into our personality. Journaling at this time of the month allows for a new perspective, a different kind of introspection and wisdom.

Finally, the dark moon is a wonderful time to look into the void, into the unknown, to find the truth hidden in the darkness. This is the time to work on psychic powers or past-life memories to help better understand current difficulties. If nothing else, it is a perfect time for divination. Look up when the moon is at its darkest and gather your favorite divinatory tool and a journal. For me, it's tarot cards, but I have also had excellent results with the pendulum, especially when doing past-life work. The most important part of divination is, at the outset, asking a question. "Should" and "will" are poor openers;

it's better to tap into the deity's special ability to know far more than you ever could and ask for information. "What is the most likely outcome?" is an excellent question, or "Tell me about *X*." But my personal favorite is "What do I need to know right now?" Then lay out your cards, dangle your pendulum, throw the bones, dice, or runes, and listen to what deity has to say to you. Follow the tangled path through the hedgerow and onto another plane. Thread the maze back through your lives, following karmic ties and patterns to unravel the meaning of what you need to know now to understand underlying patterns you didn't see previously.

Dark Moon Spell to Bring Balance

You will need:

- A round mirror at least 6 inches in diameter

- 3 small black taper candles

- A small cauldron or fireproof container

- A mixture of the following herbs: clove, mugwort, and wormwood (totalling about a large palm's worth)

- A small piece of parchment paper

- A writing instrument

Turn off all the lights. The only light should come from natural sources. Cast your circle as usual, and place the round mirror on the center of your altar. Place the three black candles in a triangle around the mirror, one candle at the top and the others at the left and right bottom of the mirror. Place your cauldron in the center of the mirror. Sprinkle the herb mixture in and around the cauldron. Light the three candles. Take several slow, deep breaths and ease into a meditative state. Reach out to your personal deities or spirit guides and ask them to guide you in examining your own dark nature. Go within and examine your personality. Look at your habits or addictions, as well as anything you may feel ashamed of or embarrassed about. What aspects of yourself do you hide from others, and why? Don't rush this process; it needs time. Write "Healing and Balance" on the piece of parchment paper. Hold the paper in your hands and say:

Darkness around me, darkness within,
In darkness comes healing, balance begins.
Child of the gods I am, in the dark moon's light,
My life is a dance of darkness and light.

Light the paper on fire and place it in the cauldron, burning some of the herbs in the cauldron as well. (Make sure the paper is burned completely.) Allow the three candles to burn down completely on their own, taking the appropriate fire-safety precautions.

Past-Life Tarot Spread

A past-life tarot spread I have worked with for several decades uses four cards and comes from a conversation I had with the astrologer P. J. Tyler, who first told me about the North and South Nodes and their link to our past lives. Card 1 represents a major unresolved (karmic) issue from a past life. Card 2 represents a hidden element of your present life that relates to the incident of card 1. Card 3 represents the outcome of this karmic issue if you do nothing further. If it is a negative outcome, draw a fourth card. Card 4 can show you how to pay your karmic debt and resolve this issue.

. . . .

Working with the dark of the moon is to work with her hidden side—and your own. It is a time to travel the inner curve of the spiral, to work with our shadow self, and to plant the seeds that will manifest at the moon's fullness. It is a path as old as our time on earth and as familiar as the stars glowing in the moonless sky. I wish you deep knowledge in your journey!

Lisa Mc Sherry is a priestess and author living in the Pacific Northwest with her husband and furchildren. She is the author of The Virtual Pagan and Magickal Connections: Creating a Lasting & Healthy Spiritual Group. The leader of JaguarMoon Coven (www.jaguarmoon.org), she is also the editor for Facing North (www.facingnorth.net), a site for reviews of interest to the Pagan/New Age/alternative spirituality community.

Illustrator: Tim Foley

Sabbats Out of Season: What to Do When You Live Where the Seasons Do Not Shift

Diana Rajchel

Southern Hemisphere Pagans who honor the sabbat wheel know the problems well: Sweltering while images of snowy Santa Claus overtake the Internet. Staring at dried leaf crafts for altar decoration while spring plants bloom outside. Shivering while reading Midsummer sabbat recipes for gazpacho. For those in the Southern Hemisphere, a simple reversal of the calendar helps: Samhain equals Beltane, and Yule equals Midsummer.

For those of us who live close enough to the equator where seasons either don't happen or happen very subtly, turning the wheel to the opposite setting does not work. The popular sabbat wheel is based on a four-season model that includes behaviors from deciduous trees that don't happen as consistently at central latitudes. For instance, in San Francisco, October 31 marks the tapering of the warmest two months of the year. Plants bloom year round. While rain can sometimes di-

vide one half of the year from the other, during droughts there is no division between periods of warmth and cold to recognize.

The living and dying Lord becomes fuzzier when you live someplace where nothing dies on a reliable schedule. People who live in regions with four seasons consciously and unconsciously plan their year around the rest periods offered by the extremes of the hot and cold seasons. Yet when neither intense cold nor intense heat are part of the climate, that inherent rhythm seems to disappear. It doesn't actually disappear; there's still a beat and rhythm. It's just that it comes from a new song of seasons. It can takes months or even years of observation to align your rhythm with that of a new climate.

Look to the Year-Round Eternal Cycles

If you are determined to stick to the sabbat wheel, there are ways to recognize and connect to the wheel energy of the place where you live. Light, tides, and the moon function on their own universal schedule. Local cultures develop their own seasons with related slowdowns and rushes in tune with ancestral and seasonal celebrations. Learning those practices can make all the difference in how you connect to your new home.

The shifting of light may happen at different angles across the globe, but each equinox and solstice distributes light the same way at the same point in time. At the winter solstice, the dark comes early, even in warm areas. As the earth changes angle, the light creeps back month by month, until spring comes and the light lingers later into the night. Connecting to the rhythms of light and dark can help you cultivate an awareness anchored in the sun.

If you live close to the ocean, the tides and the behavior of the seas display seasons of their own. Rough seas tend to happen most during winter months. In North America, December through February sees a drop in cruises on the Pacific and surfers in the water, because the ocean becomes too wild for play. This is a time of caution, just like winter in lands of ice and snow.

To connect to the push and pull of the tide, connect to the moon. Marking time month by month allows you to break down your experience into more digestible chunks. Observing a lunar calendar can ease the mental pressure that builds up when you attempt to add a solar holiday calendar to that mix.

As the earth rotates around the sun, the star patterns change. In the Northern Hemisphere, Orion's belt shines down during the winter months. Pay attention to subtle changes in the nighttime atmosphere as you spot the constellations.

Observe

Even desert climates have seasons; they just play out in a subtler way than they do in temperate climates. The hard part of learning those patterns is that you must be in them to recognize them.

While building your relationship to regional seasons, it may help to use a weather tracking app and make note of temperature, barometric pressure, and precipitation. In one state, the temperature alone may tell you if you need to turn on the air conditioner. In other areas, humidity indicates more accurately than heat whether to do so.

Allergy sufferers are already intimately familiar with another pattern to track: pollen count. Those with smartphones can download apps that inform users not just of the amount of pollen in the atmosphere but also the types of pollen most prevalent that day. This adds a layer of seasonal recognition by indicating which native plants pollinate at what time. You can further attune yourself to the new reality of a sabbat season by observing which animals mate and when they give birth. The cycles of conception and nascence establish an even more detailed seasonal schedule.

Look within the Mysteries

Each sabbat has at its core an emotional experience, a parallel that links the life and death of humanity to the life and death of plants. We grow, blossom, wither, and die at a different pace than do plants—but we do it all the same. Understanding the emotional core allows you to celebrate seasons of the soul. Meditating on each holiday and its associated myths can help you recognize spiritual themes to practice in your new environment.

Samhain

Above all, this is a time of endings, especially endings of life. This period of time calls for ending old projects, sreaching out to community members for help in tough times, and taking time alone to meditate on your choices and relationships. Reflect on what is eternal—what is the same everywhere, no matter what? Ancestors play a role in this connection, as do stories of gods, taxes, life, and death.

Yule

This season is about celebrating hope and reaching out to your community after a time of withdrawal. This does not mean we deny the darkness in the world—the winter solstice is always the longest night of the year. Acknowledging the pain and hunger that the long night brings for many in the world is one of the motivators for extending a hand to help others.

Imbolc

This sabbat is about seeding both healing and creative energies so they expand into the coming season. Its historical association with lambing season aligns it with the very beginnings of rebirth. Even if no one raises lambs near you, the symbolism can still apply. It is a time to begin projects intended to make life easier, whether that is making candles or seeking improved medical care.

Ostara

While this sabbat is commonly described as a time of rebirth, birthing has often already happened, and this is really a time of emergence for both mothers and their young. People who withdrew during the darker months now shift back to greater social interaction and reaching out to one another. There is a shift from introspection to extroversion, as the soul seeks communal connection. Projects started at Imbolc begin to show progress.

Beltane

Yes, this sabbat is about spring finally starting to blossom and about sex and sensuality. This is a time to look to the things that delight you and to nurture a sense of joy within yourself. That joy can include connection to others, and in more forms than just erotic pleasure.

Litha

This day, when the light burns the brightest, also has a great deal of eroticism attached to it, but it comes with the bittersweet awareness that all things must end. The sun sets a little earlier each day from now until the winter solstice. This happens whether the weather is hot or cold. Look for things that give you both joy and sadness, moments in your heart that at the time seemed like a wonderful forever that ended all too soon.

Lughnasadh

On this day, celebrate accomplishments, projects just starting to bear fruit. The first of two or three harvest celebrations (depending on how you view Samhain), this is the time to consider your accomplishments in life—career, love, children. Look at what you enjoyed cultivating and use this time to weed out what brought you failure, or success without joy.

MABON

Typically the middle of harvest season, when people clear fields and gardens in earnest, this is a time of assessment and preparation. What in your life can you do without—and perhaps benefit from removing from your load? What can you do at this time to provide a cushion for hard times, such as bad weather, financial difficulty, or sickness? What future would you like to have—and what can you do at this time to prepare for that?

. . . .

When you move to a new climate, temperatures may feel out of step with what a calendar calls "spring" and precipitation may throw off your sense of night and day. You can change your calendar to reflect the seasons of another culture, or you can simply reset your sabbat clock to focus on the inner experience rather than on external changes.

Diana Rajchel *is a third degree Wiccan priestess in the Shadowmoon tradition. She fills Pagan infrastructure gaps with services to people of all spiritualties relating to life, death, birth, and peace of mind. Author of* Divorcing a Real Witch *and books on Mabon and Samhain, she has written on topics relating to Paganism and the occult since 1999. Rajchel is also an experienced tarot reader, has a lively interest in how American folk magic like hoodoo can apply to modern life, and is fascinated by modern urbanism and how magical lifestyles fit with it. At present, she lives in the San Francisco Bay Area with her partner.*

Illustrator: Kathleen Edwards

Magical Transformations

Everything Old Is New Again

What to Do When You Are Called Upon

Blake Octavian Blair

If you've been in the magickal community for more than a short while, then you've likely gotten a call. You can't really refer to it as "the call," because no two are ever quite the same despite occasional shared similarities. Oftentimes, it comes in the middle of the night, or when you're on your way out to something else. Somebody needs help, counsel, divination, advice, healing work, or a shoulder to cry on. You might be thinking, *I'm not prepared to handle this,* or even, *Why did they choose to call me?* Well, in this piece we will try to face these questions head-on and explore what to do when you are called upon.

You are likely to wonder at times, at least initially, *Why did they choose to call upon me?* Well, first and foremost, chances are you are somebody they trust. You may also be in a position of leadership, chosen or unchosen. Perhaps you're the organizer of your study group or the informal leader or host of sabbat gatherings. The per-

son may know you offer tarot readings or other divination services. You might simply be well respected in your community. It could be that you have chosen (or the divine chose you—we know how that works!) a role that you knew would bring people to you, such as in one of the healing arts or the priest/esshood. However, many people who do not formally or consciously choose such roles end up in one in an informal capacity.

So what do you do now? What is your role in this situation? In the end it doesn't matter if you asked to be called upon; the fact is that you are being called upon. Feel honored that the person is comfortable enough with you and thinks highly enough of you to trust you in this situation. Certainly we want to help such people who are in a time of need. A good first step is to figure out, as respectfully and as fully as possible, what the details of the situation are. While we can't force anybody to share more than they are willing to divulge, the more we know, the more we will be able to help them appropriately. Otherwise, it is almost impossible to see what help we can offer. It is important to approach the person with calmness and compassion. If they are already emotionally fragile and borderline (or not so borderline) hysterical, it will only escalate the situation if we are in the same state.

Keep in mind that the problems or questions people bring to you can range from minor to major. Perhaps they are worried about an upcoming college exam or how to deal with a relative with whom they have a strained relationship. Perhaps they want to know the best course of action to pursue a goal. Maybe they are in an abusive relationship and need help developing an exit strategy. Perhaps a loved one is in the dying process or has just passed. The possibilities are endless. Many of us are familiar with a popular theory that the universe brings us people to help who have problems that mirror situations that are occurring or have occurred in our own lives. This creates a sort of learning lesson for us; however, the upside to this is that if it is something we have already experienced, then we have already had some preparation to help this person who now seeks our perspective. There is often wisdom in experience.

After we calmly learn the scope of the person's situation, it is time to explore exactly how we can help. A few points need to be addressed. The first is, what exactly does this person need? Simply a tarot consultation? Some friendly confidential advice? Do they need legal help and advice, perhaps from a lawyer? Are they in a dangerous abusive situation and need a shelter and professional psychological counseling? Do they need to seek a professional medical opinion? We have to decide what role we are qualified to fulfill for this person. A priest or priestess may well be qualified to offer spiritual counsel but not be certified and licensed to provide psychological treatment. Many of us are available to provide a listening ear, seasoned advice, or a shoulder to cry on. However, few of us are qualified to give legal advice. If the person needs a type of assistance that we are not legally qualified or certified to give, it is our ethical duty to refer them to someone who is qualified. This is true for many things, whether legal, medical, psychological, or other.

Something I was taught in my ministerial training that was a great piece of advice was to keep a file or recipe card box full of business cards of professionals you can refer people to. This includes everything from GLBT advocates and centers to counselors, psychologists, suicide hotlines, women's shelters, homeless shelters, healing arts practitioners, the public health department and free clinics, and other magickal people who offer services. If you don't have a business card—for the health department, for example—use a blank index card and create an info card.

One of the most noble, ethical, and professional ways you can be of help to somebody is to realize when the problem is out of your area of expertise and refer them to someone more qualified to provide the type of help needed. Furthermore, it's a great way to be of service if you can assist the person coming to you in finding that help. Even as magickal persons, we all have different strengths to offer. For example, a Reiki practitioner in the community may feel that someone who comes to them may benefit from or be in need of shamanic healing, such as a soul retrieval, and refer them to me since they do not perform the procedure. An alternate scenario is that if someone comes to me and is being abused physically or otherwise by another person, I will refer them to the proper health and legal professionals to deal with that. I'll certainly say a prayer and light a candle for their well-being, but the situation calls for far more than spiritual assistance. A far more lighthearted example given to me by a priestess friend is the time a man contacted her because he was concerned that malevolent spirits were infesting his home. He complained that rogue spirits were banging on the pipes and causing plumbing issues. From the man's description of the symptoms of the problem, she told him by all means to smudge, light a candle, and say a prayer, but also to please call a plumber!

Ultimately, our role as the one who is called upon is to ensure that the person coming to us receives the help they need, whether it ultimately is from us or not.

Ultimately, our role as the one who is called upon is to ensure that the person coming to us receives the help they need, whether it ultimately is from us or not. Next, let's discuss a few common reasons people might call upon you.

Minor to Moderate Life Situations

This is a broad category of issues. It covers anything from anxiety over an upcoming test to frustrations with friends or coworkers. These types of things can often be worked through by talking with the person and providing a listening ear, perhaps looking into the situation with a bit of divination or helping the person with a bit of relaxation from a healing modality such as Reiki. You likely will be able to help this person through some or all of these channels as a magickal person, but if not, refer them to an appropriate practitioner and/or professional.

Major Life Events or Transitions

Births, deaths, weddings, and other rites of passage can fall in this category. Some events may be joyous, such as the birth of a new family member, which could call for you to do a baby blessing and perhaps also give advice, if requested, on how to integrate the new child into the family unit.

Perhaps it is a wedding you are being asked to officiate. Many Pagan weddings, in my experience as a minister, have a higher chance of being just a small ceremony with some intimate friends, family, and spiritual community members. Whether this is because many blood relatives disagree with their relationship or religion, because they wish to keep costs down, or simply because they prefer a smaller setting, I find that magickally minded weddings tend to have fifty or fewer attendees. This often means that, as clergy, you not only are filling the role of officiant but are also helping to plan the ceremonial and ritual elements. They aren't likely to have a planner coordinating all aspects of the ceremony. This is significant, as the wedding is the outward spiritual expression to the universe of a most intimate and important part of their lives, and they are entrusting you with it. As the minister/officiant who weds the two people, you have an energetic connection to the couple simply by performing the ceremony. You may or may not be qualified to officiate a wedding. That will depend on your training and credentials. If needed, refer them to

somebody qualified. It is important to remember, though, that these joyous events need the approach of a caring, compassionate soul just as much as does a more heart-wrenching event, such as a death.

You might be called upon by somebody to assist with the death of a loved one. Your assistance may be desired not only after a loved one has passed but also during the process of the person's passing. Many spiritual traditions include death rites and preparations for a person still living, and you might be called upon to facilitate such rites. If you are qualified, it is an honor to be asked to participate in someone's life at such a personal time. If you are not, you can still be a compassionate friend and supportive community member and refer them to a qualified practitioner. The dying person as well as their loved ones will all benefit from your support and compassion at this time.

Coming Out

GLBT

You may be approached by someone who needs support or advice regarding coming out of the closet as gay, lesbian, bisexual, or transgender. Coming out can be a time of both joy and trepidation. Although we have a long way to go in many areas of society, acceptance does seem to be progressing, thankfully. It is becoming more and more common at younger and younger ages for people to feel comfortable and desire to live freely and openly. This also holds true for older persons who identify as being under the GLBT umbrella. Many people who have been in the closet for decades now are seeing enough support to have the strength and fortitude to let the world know who they truly are. Because faiths that fall somewhere under the Pagan and earth-centered umbrella tend to be generally very GLBT-affirming, we tend to attract a fair number of people who are also under the GLBT umbrella. You may have people in this situation come to you whether you yourself are GLBT or not; however, you may be more likely to encounter this if you are GLBT as well.

Spiritual Broom Closet

If you've been around the Pagan block a few years, you've more than likely already had a person who is in the broom closet come to you. One scenario is that they have ruminated for a long time about their spirituality and have found their way, as we once did, to a place under the Pagan umbrella, and in the process they have wandered into your sphere. Another common scenario is that they were not Pagan but were associated with you in some way, and now they have decided they identify best with a similar set of beliefs.

In either case, you are likely very qualified to help this person. We've all been in their shoes at one point or another, whether it was just a few or many years ago. Such people have much to be guided through, from how to approach relatives to where to find reliable information and how to integrate themselves into the greater Pagan community. Without friends of like mind, it can be a very lonely place, and you can help prevent that from being their experience. Point them toward your favorite open gatherings and perhaps go with them, suggest favorite publications, and just be a good friend.

Sadly, in this day and age, many people are still persecuted for their religious beliefs in our society. So a strong sense of community is very important, especially for those of us in faiths that are not the culturally dominant strain in most of society.

Crisis and Trauma

Those who are seen as wise guides are often approached by people who are experiencing various life traumas. Perhaps they are recently or long-term unemployed, an experience that can be soul-depleting and draining to go through. Maybe they were in a major auto accident and are recovering from physical and emotional trauma. They could be experiencing some stark facts about the aging process, including being not necessarily disabled but less abled than they used to be. While we may not be qualified to offer them legal, medical, or psychological advice or treatment, we have our spiritual perspectives and moral support to offer. Many people love to throw around the old adage "This too shall pass." While that may be true, it may not always feel like it to a person going through a traumatic period. Be a friend to them while it passes. That is what they truly need.

. . . .

The potential situations in which people may seek your assistance are as varied and unique as the individuals who are experiencing them. The best you can do is be prepared and bring to the situation a bit of wisdom, a ton of compassion, and any skills and qualifications you may have (magickal or mundane), and be ready with a referral if necessary. Sometimes all it takes is a cup of tea, twenty minutes of Reiki, and a short oracle card reading. Other situations call for a lot more.

Some of the advice in this article might seem a bit mundane to you. However, as magickal people we are often termed "walkers between the worlds." Well, to earn that title, we must master these mundane matters (to the best of our abilities—we are perpetually growing and learning) so that when they arise, we can help our friends, magickally minded and not so magickally minded. Another important point to remember is that we often say the first step to working successful magick is taking action in the mundane world. Support your magick. For example, all the job spells in the world will not help you gain employment if you do not network, apply for jobs, and show up to the interviews. The spell functions as a magickal boost to those actions.

To help another when you are called upon is truly magickal in and of itself—in the lives of those who come to you and in your own life. For what you put into the universe, I believe you get back. When you call upon somebody, may they in turn be there for you!

Blake Octavian Blair *is an eclectic Pagan, ordained minister, shamanic practitioner, writer, Usui Reiki Master-Teacher, tarot reader, and musical artist. Blake blends various mystical traditions from both the East and West along with a reverence for the natural world into his own brand of modern Paganism and magick. Blake holds a degree in English and Religion from the University of Florida. He is an avid reader, crafter, and practicing pescatarian. He loves communing with nature and exploring its beauty whether it is within the city or hiking in the woods. Blake lives in the New England region of the USA with his beloved husband. Visit him on the web at www.blakeoctavianblair.com or write him at blake@blakeoctavianblair.com.*

Illustrator: Jennifer Hewitson

Children of the Reeds: Adventures in a Not-So-Imaginary Place

Linda Raedisch

An ordinary place exists only on the map, while a sacred place exists half in the imagination. It's a little more difficult to say what sets a sacred place apart from an imaginary place. Perhaps the difference exists only in the imagination. My own sacred place exists within the Great Swamp of north central New Jersey. It was at the newly developed edge of these wetlands that one of the most mysterious encounters of my life took place, though I did not see it as mysterious at the time.

I was about four years old, an age at which much of life is still a mystery. When I think of my early childhood, the swamp looms large: the sibilant rustling of Phragmites—around here the common reed goes by its taxonomic name—and the pungent blue burning of my father's cigar, which, he told me, he  smoked to keep the deer flies and mosquitoes at bay. In those days, I liked nothing better than to pack a bag of peanut butter sandwiches and walk with him along one of the dirt roads that ran the length of "our" stretch of swamp. At one end of the road was the busy thoroughfare leading to my sister's school, and at the other, a housing development in the throes of construction. Even from deep in the reeds you could hear the clatter of hammers and the raw ringing of power saws. The houses going up were much larger than ours: four and five bedrooms with dressing rooms, playrooms, and dens. A few were already lived in, while others were mere frameworks open to the sky.

The streets themselves were brand-new too, and it was while exploring the freshly tarred Crocodile Drive that I spotted the children: a brown-haired girl and a brown-haired boy, both about my own age, playing in a sandbox installed among the rust brown rocks and swamp clay of their desolate new yard. We regarded one another in silence. They did not ask me to stop and play, nor was I sure I wanted them to. Soon, my father and I had passed on up the hill to return home along the shoulder of the main road.

Those children held a strange fascination for me. I did not go to nursery school and had no neighbors my own age. My sister, three and a half years older, was a creature of a much higher order and always seemed to be in school. Most days, children simply weren't on the menu, so I was eager to get another glimpse of those sandbox kids. Couldn't we take another walk down Crocodile Drive?

Where?

Crocodile Drive!

No such street. My father and I continued to include the development in our swampy ramblings, but there simply was no Crocodile Drive, only hard-packed earth and a thicket of native laurel where the children and the sandbox should have been. I was not overly troubled by this state of affairs at the time, not with so many other mysteries to occupy my growing mind. Eventually I, too, got to go to school; not the old brick school where my sister had started but the new open-plan experiment through whose large, paneless windows I could look down on my old stomping grounds, at the hummocks, the purple-horned skunk cabbages, and the occasional flash of a red-winged blackbird's epaulette among the Phragmites.

I learned about places far beyond my swamp, places impossibly distant in time and space. In seventh grade, I developed a fascination for all things ancient, especially the civilization of Sumer. Had I expressed this fascination more openly, and had life been a little different, there might have been trips to museums and libraries to see the artifacts close up, to learn more. But life was not like that, and my love for ancient Sumer remained an intensely personal matter, as personal as my love for the swamp.

And, for a time, my swamp became Sumer. The cracked clay deposits in the ruts of the dirt paths provided the clay with which the first scribe (me!) formed the first cuneiform tablets. The brown, slow-moving streams became the Tigris and Euphrates. The feathery stands of Phragmites along their banks were the reed thickets of Eridu, site

of the world's first city. I gave little thought to the fact that at the same time my swamp was becoming my Sumer, Sumer itself was a land lost to time, its brick temples eroded to soft mounds, the reed thickets silted up with salt and sand.

Once upon a time, that land between two rivers had been an eden, *the* Eden, for *eden* was the Sumerian word for the fertile alluvial plain on which they built their cities. For the Sumerians, it was simply home. The Sumerian paradise, on the other hand, was a land called Dilmun, a place of eternal life and freedom from suffering, a sacred realm where "the raven utters no cry." In the 1960s, it was discovered that Dilmun was also a real place, a civilization on a par with those of Mesopotamia and centered on the island of Bahrain. Dilmun, then, like my own personal Sumer, was both a place you could point to on a map and one that existed only on the plains of the imagination.

I no longer live within earshot of those whispering Phragmites; I'm about a five-minute drive from that dirt service road, and, I have to admit, I no longer visit all that often. And yet I'm always aware of where I am in relation to the swamp. In the early afternoon, when the sun first shines from the direction of the swamp, I find myself stopping in the patch of light falling through the window as if to say hello. I've since had adventures much further afield and in far more impressive landscapes, but the swamp remains my sacred place and I think I will never live far from it, at least not for long.

And what about Crocodile Drive? Over the years, a few more roads have made incursions into the reeds and laurel thickets. I've walked up and down them and none of them is Crocodile Drive. It was not until about ten years ago, after I had embarked on the study of the folklore of fairies, that I began to view the sandbox children in a different light. Like the old-time "good people," or fairies, they had looked perfectly ordinary, were of a higher station than I was, had appeared on the border between wilderness and human settlement, and had disappeared without a trace. I'll never know exactly who or what they were, but I sometimes wonder if I presented as much of a mystery to them as they did to me. Perhaps, even now, one of them is composing an essay about the time they saw a pale blond fairy child emerge from the swamp, stroll past the yard, then vanish into thin air…

Linda Raedisch *is the author of* The Old Magic of Christmas: Yuletide Traditions for the Darkest Days of the Year (*Llewellyn, 2013*) *as well as numerous articles on folklore, ethnobotany, archaeology, and religion. She is currently at work on a book about the origins of the witch figure. You can find her on Facebook or simply look for the house with the witch's hat on the lamppost.*

Illustrator: Neil Brigham

Why You Need Your Muse

Deborah Castellano

If you're not an artist, a musician, or a writer, you might think you don't have a muse. Wrong. Everyone does. Just because yours is different from the media portrayal of the muse doesn't mean she* doesn't exist. What media portrayal currently describes your struggles and your life right now? What, none? Exactly.

My mom's muse can't be bothered with airy-fairy artiste junk. She barfs up snarled balls of yarn full of knotted and

---

*I have chosen "she" as the third person neutral for this piece because that's what's organic for me. Feel free to insert whatever pronoun you like.

tangled tax code. It's up to my mom (and her muse) to wrangle that hot mess into order. My mom's muse answers to the name Mrs. Emma Peel and dreams in numbers.

The character of Don Draper is frequently seen as the Establishment on the TV show *Mad Men*. He's full of hetero white-guy privilege during a time when it was extra tasty and delicious to be a hetero white guy due to the buckets of money, ease of middle-class life, and all the underpaid female labor there to help you at the office and at home. Don's a brilliant ad man, and his words and images evoke beauty and longing, which is very useful when you're in advertising. His muse creates artistic advertising with him.

What Do You Dream About?

What is your Great Work? Take some time to ponder that question, as it will define your relationship with your muse. I don't feel everyone's Great Work is necessarily based in the pursuit of occult knowledge. Maybe your Great Work is in the occult arts, but maybe it isn't. Maybe it's math, maybe it's science, maybe it's cooking, maybe it's cleaning, maybe it's flying a plane, maybe it's making a really fantastic cup of coffee. But it's in there, in you. Where is the heart of your passion? What would you regret not accomplishing in your life? Distill this into one sentence. You can work on other quests later, but for now, content yourself with identifying just one.

What is your Great Work? Take some time to ponder that question, as it will define your relationship with your muse.

Meet Your Muse

Muses are slippery creatures by nature. While the muse is often referred to as a female, there is no reason yours can't be male or some other gender altogether. One thing most muses have in common is that they tend to be very clear about who is the dominant party in the relationship. Here's a hint: it's not you.

Have you met your muse yet? If not, it's going to be a lot of work getting to her. Not impossible, by any means, but work. Chances are she's been asleep at the wheel for a while. If you've already met your muse, chances are your relationship with her is not optimal, which is why you're attempting to develop a more open and honest connection with her. That will be even harder, as she's likely irritated with you.

Let's start with the first scenario: that you haven't met your muse yet. On a Friday, pour out a libation that you think your muse will like best, whether that's champagne, Red Bull, Scotch, pomegranate juice, Clamato juice, or a cup of tea. Your muse is a part of you (and you are a part of her), so this is a scenario in which you honestly know best. Put out a small plate of treats for your muse. This could be cherries wrapped in prosciutto, a marrow bone, or a glorious piece of chocolate. Take a small pink candle and light it with your

intent to commune with your muse. Write on a piece of joss paper (sold in Asian supermarkets) why you want to be friends with your muse. Don't let your pen leave the paper as you write; if it does, start over. (You will end up with a lot of loops when you dot the i's and cross the t's.) Roll the paper toward you with a little ginger powder dusted on it, then light the paper in the candle and let it burn in a heat-safe container, such as your cauldron.

Wait a week to see if you get any feedback. Did you hear a specific song repeatedly on the radio, in the supermarket, and in your playlist? Did you see some kind of omen that wasn't there before, like seven bunnies in every empty field you passed? Did your muse appear to you in a dream or in your meditation work? At two o'clock in the morning was that royal pain kicking your bed with a brilliant but inconvenient idea? If so, then you've made contact. Congratulations! You're on your way to a more interesting life.

If you haven't heard from your muse in a week, then obviously she didn't like your presents. She's a vegan, she thinks cherries are gross, she doesn't eat sugar anymore, gluten makes her stomach cramp, or whatever. Or maybe she's playing hard to get. That's a fun game muses like to play. In that case, continue offering different things on a Friday with a new candle and a new petition, waiting a week for her reply, until your muse shows up. Usually this approach is not one that I recommend with the goddesses and spirits (as well as humans), because sometimes, friend, they're just not that into you. That level of persistence is stalkeresque, which is a turn-off in 99 percent of the situations you will find yourself in. But this is an exception to the rule—because your muse is a piece of you and you are a piece of your muse. Due to that symbiotic relationship, it's fine *in this one particular case* to chase your muse like a lovesick puppy—because it means you're also chasing yourself (and running away from yourself) like a lovesick puppy, which will blow the doors off your brain when you get deeply involved enough with your muse.

Here's something to remember: while, yes, your muse is a part of you and you are part of her, she's still also her own spirit/being. Take your muse's cues and do not antagonize her for the sake of antagonizing her, because it's just going to make everything more difficult for both of you in the long run. Trust me.

Rekindle Your Bond with Your Muse

If you've already met your muse and you're reading this, chances are she ditched you. She climbed out the restaurant's bathroom window while she claimed to be powdering her nose. It is possibly even more challenging to get in touch with your muse if you've already met her and she's given you the slip because—surprise!—she's annoyed with you. How do you know if your muse has checked out and is no longer responding to your calls? Well, have you been devoid of inspiration? Have you been stubbornly sticking to a routine that leaves no room for creativity and thus no room for your muse? If so, that means you're too boring to bother with. You need to spice up the relationship again.

To figure out where your muse has been hiding, let her know you're looking for her by nightly stating your intention out loud that you want to find her. When you start receiving omens that she has

received your intention, you need to begin wooing her back by making offerings to her (as outlined previously) until you receive omens that she has returned to your life.

That will not be enough for your relationship to be saved, however. You are going to need to offer her a sacrifice. Chances are she's really aggravated with you, which is why she dumped your rump like a bad habit. People, spirits, and goddesses like a pound of flesh when they feel wronged by you; it's just the nature of anger. The good news is you probably won't have to give her an actual pound of flesh. The bad news is it's called a sacrifice for a reason.

I can't speak for your muse any more than I can speak for, say, all women everywhere, but I can tell you that my muse likes the sacrifice of time, routine, and money best. As I get older, I get more tight-fisted and regimented about all of the aspects that make her roll her eyes so hard she could be in a television teen drama. I'm a writer, so my muse is completely uninterested in what I need to do to survive and be mentally stable. Working, being in a long-term relationship, paying off bills, maintaining a home, and staying in most weekends? Booooooooring! She doesn't want to be bothered with the petty details of how I maintain my existence; she wants to eat waffles while wearing an expensive men's shirt after a night at a gala and then have me write about how witty, charming, and clever she is.

As a writer, it's hard to write exciting things if your life isn't terribly interesting, which is likely part of your muse's motivation. It's hard to dream of new, exciting worlds when you're too weighed down by the laundry that has to be done in this one.

Am I saying that you should give in to every demand your muse makes of you, as if you were some kind of slave? Do you conduct any relationship in your life like that? Um, no. Learn how to negotiate.

My muse may want the life of an Upper East Sider in New York City, but she's attached to a suburban girl from New Jersey. I don't have the means or the connections to truly give her the kind of life she wants. So we negotiate. Going to see an electric cello ensemble concert was a sacrifice she found acceptable, as it had the elements she likes: time (schlepping out to Philly after a week of ten-hour work days when I was exhausted), money (cost of drinks, transportation, and new fishnet stockings), and effort (I could have gone in a little black dress, but I went all out in my most elegant gothic wear, and dancing is not as easy as it once was for me). Voilà!

Sounds lovely and fun, right? Sometimes part of your sacrifice will be nonconsensual; that's why it's called a sacrifice. My muse likes to punch me where it hurts when she's mad at me. After the concert, she also took two paying gigs out from under me at the very last minute. Our relationship is always contentious, though yours doesn't have to be with your muse.

Sacrifices to Your Muse

First, think about your muse. How do you see your muse? What is she like? What does she look like? How does your muse communicate with you typically? How would you describe your relationship with your muse?

Now think about your personal Great Work. What are you trying to accomplish and why?

With that information (and, ideally, feedback from your muse), think about what would be a good sacrifice. Time, money, and effort are common modern-day sacrifices. And there's always a *gaes*, which is when you and your muse come to an agreement that you will do (or not do) X or Y thing for Z amount of time. The easiest modern example of this would be when a Catholic gives something up for the forty days of Lent. A gaes is a vow. If you make a vow to a spirit or a god, you better mean it, because bad things will quickly follow if you don't. So make sure you mean it and it's something you can accomplish. You'll know your sacrifice was accepted when you start to see movement in your Great Work and/or feel (divinely) inspired. Until then, keep sacrificing and contacting until you get somewhere.

Why Go to All This Trouble to Work With Your Muse?

That's an excellent question. If you want to see extraordinary results in your Great Work, then you need to be willing to work hard. Collaborating with a muse is hard. For one thing, your muse doesn't see it as collaborating. If you think you can completely control your muse,

you are *hilarious*. That's like saying you can completely control your mother.

So why deal with the unknown and the untamed? Why potentially be burned? Um, why do you do magic? Your relationship with your muse is magical, like any relationship with a spirit. Most people choose not to do magic or commune with spirits. Many people spend much of their lives on Facebook and playing Candy Crush. Do you want to spend most of your life on Facebook and playing Candy Crush or do you want to get somewhere? Right.

Too Much! Too Much!

So you did everything you were supposed to do and the results are more than you're prepared to handle. You reached your goal, but now you're feeling overwhelmed. First, make sure that you really want to put the brakes on this. Are you just feeling scared and overworked? As I can tell you from experience, your lizard brain hates fear and uncertainty and will do just about anything to convince you to go back to the status quo.

Take a sick day and pretend like you're going to live a normal human life like a normal human being for a day. After that day, reassess the situation and remind your lizard brain that you didn't come here to be a normal human.

Still not ready? Even the fiercest Witch has moments of weakness. It's time for you to regroup and give your muse the slip for a while.

For the next two weeks, you are to have the most boring, mundane life possible. Go back to how you were living when *she* gave *you* the slip in the first place. Eat boring food, go to work, watch television at home, do laundry, don't have any sex, and don't do anything creative or fun. Fly under the radar until things settle down enough for you to ride the tiger again.

Then get to it!

Deborah Castellano *writes for many of Llewellyn's annuals and has a blog on PaganSquare where she gives unsolicited opinions on glamour, the Muse, and the occult. Her online shop, The Mermaid & The Crow, specializes in handmade goods. She resides in New Jersey with her husband, Jow, and two cats. She has a terrible reality-television habit she can't shake and likes St. Germain liqueur, record players, and typewriters. Visit her at www.deborahmcastellano.com.*

Illustrator: Rik Olson

Opening Divine Dialogue: Personal Healing with the Ancient Ones

Tiffany Lazic

Under a moonless sky in a home-made crystal cave at a time of seeking, three figures approach: one woman to be, one woman who has been, and a goddess. Crones all three, and each bearing a message. Or rather, the same message told three different ways. I recognize the woman who has been. It is my mom, who has dwelt many years now in Summerland. The woman to be is somewhat recognizable as me, but she is old, wrinkled, and gray and seems not to have the same cares upon her shoulders. The goddess, though, is well known. She

is the Crone, the Hag, the Cailleach. I have seen her many times and have tried to avoid her as many times as I have turned to her. She has been sharp, unyielding, and stern. But she has also been steady, understanding, and, in her own way, deeply loving. She has always called me to bring my best, especially during those times when I wished to turn away from her.

We have many ways to connect and communicate with the gods and goddesses, those key archetypal energies that have provided guidance since time immemorial. Engaging with these energies in ritual, whether solitary or in a group, allows us to enter their stories and experience ourselves in the flow of the river of time. These themes have appeared over decades, centuries, and eons. Ritual brings the timeless to today. We step into it and awaken our mythic dimension in the context of our greater community and the cycles that touch us all.

But there is a more individual and personal approach to working with the gods and goddesses. They can help us become aware of where we may have become lost to the truth of ourselves. They can guide us to shift where we are stuck or have repressed our inner strength and wisdom. They can reflect to us the best in ourselves. Transpersonal psychology works with the concept of subpersonalities. Best known through the work of Robert Assagioli (who developed an approach to psychology called psychosynthesis), Hal and Sidra Stone, and John Rowan (to name but a few), a subpersonality is the term used to describe a mask we put on in order to protect ourselves. Subpersonalities are roles we embrace to ensure our acceptance by others. If we do not feel we will be accepted just the way we are simply for being who we are, then we will engage a subpersonality to receive the attention we seek according to an unconscious belief about what we perceive to be acceptable to others. Subpersonalities are not who we are, but who we present ourselves to be to others to fulfill a very specific function.

We all have subpersonalities. They are unavoidable in a society that has such a prevalence of low self-esteem. Rooted in shame, subpersonalities are "born" in childhood in order to get our needs met. In order to gain positive attention from your parents, you may have become the Hero Child or Perfectionist. As the well-known axiom goes, "If we can't get good attention, we will settle for whatever attention we can get," and thus you may have instead become the Scapegoat Child or Rebel. As we grow into adulthood, we carry these familiar ways of being with us. We may not even recognize them as being separate from who we are, and we may believe that they are, in fact, an aspect of our true personality. Some common subpersonalities include the Caretaker, Rescuer, People-Pleaser, Approval-Seeker, Martyr, Bully, Victim, Pillar-of-Strength, Saboteur, and, of course, the almost ever-present Critic. Each subpersonality carries its own distinct stamp and functions in its own way. We may call them by different names, but the "stamp" is always recognizable. My Perfectionist may present slightly differently than your Perfectionist, but both of them are trying to cover up a deeply rooted sense of inadequacy. Both are informed by Shadow rather than Light.

Subpersonalities differ from roles we need to take on to get a particular job done or contribute to our community in some way. I may consciously take on the role of teacher because I love learning and sharing what I have discovered, but I can recognize that that is not who I am. It is a job I do that happens to be in alignment with my inner passion. With subpersonalities, we do not recognize that we have a choice in behavior. It is important to begin to distinguish between the truth of who we are at our core and the ways in which we have adapted ourselves to be acceptable.

If subpersonalities arise out of our insecurity, shame, and Shadow, then the Ancient Ones can aid in leading us back into the Light. As universal archetypes, the gods and goddesses are reflections of key divine qualities that we can reclaim within ourselves, transforming the dark we have carried for so long. Much like subpersonalities, many gods and goddesses reverberate with a similar quality, though the particularities of expression differ from culture to culture. A sun god is a

sun god, whether we call him Helios, Apollo, Lugh, Tonatiuh, or Ra. Though each one has a host of stories specific to the land from which he hails, each also reflects the message of light, vitality, courage, and energy. The tales of the Ancient Ones are not without trials and challenges. It is through their stories, as well as through the archetypal energy they carry, that we can gain insight about how to overcome our own obstacles and find the strength within to prevail.

In a list that is almost endless, what follows are some of the gods and goddesses that may be familiar, presented from the perspective of their main archetypal energy and how they can help resolve interpersonal dynamics and heal low self-esteem and shame.

The Mothers guide us to self-care and nurturing. A mother goddess knows what needs to be done to care for the life force that flows through each one of us, ensuring that our needs on all levels of being are met. She brings our attention to our physical bodies, encouraging us to nourish ourselves and get sufficient sleep and making sure we feel safe in our lives. If the mother goddess is not active within, the Caretaker subpersonality may show up. The Caretaker is far more focused on the needs of others, sacrificing herself in the process. The Caretaker believes that her worth comes from what she does for others and that if she stops taking care of others, she will be rejected. Some mother goddesses who can help heal the Caretaker and bring balance back into our lives are Gaia, Demeter, Yemaya, Hathor, Terra Mater, Danu, and Nerthus.

The Warriors guide us to come from a feeling of empowerment, anchoring within us positive self-regard, willpower, and a healthy approach to boundaries. A warrior god or goddess comes from that place of both inner and outer strength, reflecting self-confidence, self-worth, and personal power. If the warrior god or goddess is not present within, one of several subpersonalities can become evident. The Victim subpersonality experiences little personal power, seeing him- or herself as being at the mercy of other people, situations, or even life itself. On the other end of the spectrum is the Bully subpersonality, who attempts to feel worthy and significant through wresting power from others. In truth, what lies beneath the surface of the Bully is the same sense of inadequacy that informs the Victim. There are numerous warrior gods and goddesses who can help us learn to say no, express anger in a positive way, and stand up for what we know to be of intrinsic value in our lives. Some, such as Ares, Sekhmet, Kali, the Morrigan, and Thor, tend to be more forceful in approach. Some, such as Athena, Horus, and Tyr, tend to be more strategic and righteous in approach. Different situations call for different inner activations. Sometimes Athena energy just won't do the job as effectively, and Kali really is necessary.

In a world of people who are experiencing information overload, the Communicators guide us to sift the relevant from the inconsequential and to express ourselves with eloquence and integrity. Many of these deities have been credited with gifting humanity with the written word or presiding over the expressive arts. They foster a sense of trust and reliability, knowing that one of the most valuable commodities we have is our word. They urge us to speak from both the mind and the heart, acknowledging the divine in every word. When one of these gods or goddesses is not present within, one subpersonality that can arise is the Drama Queen, whose words are inflated in order to feel important. Communicating the pain of a stubbed toe can reach epic proportions if fueled by an unconscious belief that no one will care. The Silent One operates from the same belief but will endure endless pain in silence rather than risk being ignored while vulnerable. Neither of these subpersonalities speaks the truth from mind and heart, nor, in the over- or under-sharing, does either honor the individual's innate worth. The repression of the Communicators is also evident when lies, joking, deflection, veiled or hidden meanings, or duplicitous talk are present. Communicator gods and goddesses, such as Thoth, Ogma, Odin, Brigid, and Hermes, help us to recognize the sacred nature of communication and guide us to honor both ourselves and the other in the form and content of expression.

All archetypes are supported and enhanced if the Mages are present. These gods and goddesses are the conduits of intuition, providing guidance and wisdom. They help us to understand myth, metaphor, and symbols. They illuminate synchronicity in our lives so that we can feel the presence of the divine in even the smallest of occurrences. They encourage us to trust our inner sight and inner knowing, again bringing cohesion to mind and heart. And they always support us in seeing the bigger picture, knowing that our wisdom is best directed in service to ourselves, others, and the All. An inability to trust the Mages can result in the Controller subpersonality, who seldom listens to his or her feelings, striving to control situations and other people, which leads inevitably to stress and exhaustion, physically, emotionally, and mentally. We can evoke the Mages through meditation, being open to the presence of magic in our lives, and knowing ourselves to be one aspect of a far larger and immensely profound pattern. Learning a divination tool, such as tarot, is also an excellent way to connect to their energy. Isis, Ceridwen, and Hekate, goddesses of magic and transformation, are a few of the best-known and beloved Mages.

It was one of these faces of the Mage that I met that night under the moonless sky. Though at times, when she has approached me alone, I have felt her to be so strong, sure, and no-nonsense as to be

 frightening, there was something about seeing her alongside my loved and greatly missed mother and my much older self that helped me to recognize something of her in myself. The presenting trinity appeared as "Maiden, Mother, Crone." This maiden was an old woman, this mother had long left the earthly realm, and this crone was timeless, but they all reflected the same message of wisdom and guidance, with particulars specific to my challenges, blind spots, and Shadow. They each reflected the Light to illuminate my path forward.

We are born of pure Essence. We lose sight of that. We become encrusted with heaviness, negativity, and self-abnegation. That is not our purpose. Our purpose is to reflect the beauty, grace, and magic of the divine while we walk upon this earth in human form. The Ancient Ones can lead us back again. They too reflect the dicey spots where we may be led astray, but they also offer the truth of our own brilliance, if we can garner the courage to let it shine.

Tiffany Lazic *is a Registered Psychotherapist and Spiritual Director with a private practice in individual, couples, and group therapy. As the owner of the Hive and Grove Centre for Holistic Wellness, she created and teaches two self-development programs, Patterns of Conscious Living and Spiritual Language of the Divine, as well as teaching in the Transformational Arts College of Spiritual and Holistic Training's Spiritual Directorship and Divine Connections Training Programs. An international presenter and keynote speaker, Tiffany has conducted workshops for many conferences and organizations in Canada, the US, and the UK. She is a member of the Sisterhood of Avalon, where she serves on the Board of Trustees, and is the founder of Kitchener's Red Tent Temple. Tiffany is the author of* The Great Work: Self-Knowledge and Healing Through the Wheel of the Year *(Llewellyn Publications, 2015).*

Illustrator: Bri Hermanson

A Witch on the Land: Befriending the Powers of Place

Danu Forest

A Witch, a wisewoman, knows the spirits of the land around her as closely as kin, as cousins. She knows every curve of the earth—the green hillsides and the rolling fields of golden barley. She knows the trees in the woodland personally, rejoicing at the appearance of buds and seedlings as at the birth of a child. The river is her sister, the well her confidante, the wind and the rain and the wide blue sky as much her coverlet as her blanket by the fire. Her hearth is a beating heart, and her home is in every atom of soil.

Weaving into the Old Ways

In Britain, the history of venerating the spirits of the land goes back thousands of years. Dating back to the Neolithic Era, we have ancestral burial mounds known as barrows, stone circles, and rows aligned to the stars and the movements of the sun and moon. We also have sacred complexes where these sites are grouped together for ceremonial purposes, in places where the very earth itself is and was considered holy, sacred. Central to all these ancient constructions is their positioning on the landscape itself; hilltops, caves, islands, the sources of rivers, forests and single ancient trees, and panoramic views as well as naturally circular enclosed horizons have all been marked out as special. These are places where the spirits of the land make themselves known, where the land itself feels more alive. They are liminal places where the veil is thin and can be crossed at will.

By the Bronze and Iron Ages, the Celts left grand offerings at such places. They left swords and shields as honored gifts to the spirits of place, the spirits of nature. Then as Christianity came and the Old Ways were demoted to folklore, the offerings changed to bowls of cream and milk, honey, and butter for the faery folk and the "powers of place," as they're called, but the spirits remain as strong as ever.

It's the same all around the world. The cultures, traditions, and landscapes may differ, but look deeply with clear eyes at the earth around you and you will find places, even beneath the city streets, that have been held as sacred, where the spirits of the land remember when we walked hand in hand with them. They remember when we shared the green earth together as kin. With some care, some commitment, some love, and some guts, we can rekindle these friendships and gain so much more than power and spirit allies to help us with our work. We can gain a greater vision and learn to walk in rhythm with the heart of the earth herself. Then our magic is *her* magic, and our craft, *her* craft. We walk in service to something greater than ourselves, and are supported in turn by the very soul of nature.

Befriending the Spirits

For me, coming to know the spirits of place has as much to do with understanding how this landscape functions—how it changes through the seasons, its moods, the ways it expresses itself under sun and starlight—as it does with knowing its stories, its history. I now eat food grown from its rich soil, and I drink its red and white waters—sacred springs colored by their infusions of iron and calcite. To grow into relationship with the land, wherever you are, means the same things. You need to live there, draw sustenance from the earth, drink the waters there, and have its dirt under your fingernails and its grass beneath your bare feet—not just for a week or a month, but for years. If a place is truly in your heart, then it's not a long road; it's the life you live.

Learning the Land

There are so many ways to become aware of and honor the spirits of place, even those long forgotten. Start by being aware of yourself, present and conscious of the "now." Take a slow, deep breath and feel your bare feet on the earth. Close your eyes and listen. What do you hear? What do you feel? Take note of those subtle little sensations in your body—they have much to teach you about the energy and spirit of a place. Take long walks and really notice your surroundings, the lay of the land and its shapes, curves, and dips. Where are the rivers? Do they still flow as they did or have they disappeared underground? Where are the oldest trees? What is the history of your land? Who were its earliest inhabitants? Ask around, look for old photos, and visit a library. Find old wells, folk tales, and faery stories and visit their locations. Get to know every inch of your land. Be present and aware, and look out for how a place feels to your body as well as your mind and intuition—that sense in your gut, the tingle up your spine, that gust of wind just when you wonder if there are spirits here. Believe me, they are everywhere; just train yourself to notice them. And when you reach out to them, they will notice you in return.

Simple Seership

Another way to get to know the land is to "journey" or meditate. This can be as directed and deliberate as participating in a full shamanic ceremony to gain vision or as simple as sitting by your fire (as my Celtic ancestors used to do) and letting a trance come over you as gentle as rain. Close your eyes, breathe deeply, and wander the roads outside your home in your imagination. See how different it all looks using your inner eyes. Who do you meet on the spirit roads, the faery paths? Do you feel the dragon lines pulsing like the veins of the earth goddess herself? Seek quietude, stretch out your senses a little, and see for yourself. In your waking day, visit the waterways, the forest, the local park, and be open to whatever draws your attention. Notice that stone by the path. Will it be your friend and speak of the memory of the earth? The tree in the yard—will it be kin and ally to you and teach you how to grow deep roots, how to bend in the wind? Sit quietly by their side, and let your inner vision commune with them while the seasons turn and turn again. Reach out to them honestly, gently, kindly, and listen with your whole body. You may be surprised.

Walking the Spirit Roads

Dowsing is a simple and practical way to discover the spirit roads and energy vortexes in your area, which will take many forms. Sometimes a spirit road will be a traditional route taken from a village to a burial ground and will have human as well as energetic markers and presences. Others will be the deep energetic currents of earth energy in your area, the dragon lines. Ley lines are another spirit road, usually made of or marked by a line of natural or built features, such as ancient stone circles, while faery roads—those traversed often by faeries and other spirits going about their own business—may be any shape or length, often changing course or ending abruptly and only appearing at certain times of the day or year.

To dowse, you can use one of several types of dowsing tools, or you can use your own hands and inner senses if you are sensitive enough. A traditional dowsing rod, which was commonly used to find water in the British Isles until the last few centuries, is a thin hazelwood branch with a natural fork at one end. Hold the stick in both hands by the forked end, high and parallel to the ground, and walk slowly back and forth over an area. Breathe slowly, letting your mind go as blank and rested as possible. When you have found something, the stick will suddenly dip down to the ground or sometimes lurch to one side—it's usually a very tangible feeling and clearly not something you have made the stick do yourself. Be aware of any ideas, images, or other sensations you experience when doing this, as these can provide further details as to the kind of energetic feature you have found. You may be able to chart the flow or path of the spirit road by continuing to sweep across the area with your dowsing rod and noticing where the feature is and where it isn't. A modern equivalent of a hazel dowsing rod is a pair of thick copper wires bent at a right angle and used in the same way: held parallel to the ground, with one wire in each hand. When the wires have found something, they usually cross each other. Again, it will feel very clear and tangible and not like something you've done yourself by accident.

Similarly, you can use a pendulum to discover energetic features by suspending it over a map and asking it to point out areas of spirit presence or energy. Though this takes practice, it can be very helpful and can narrow down your searches.

If you are sensitive enough, you can also learn to dowse with your hands. Again, let yourself be calm and still, thinking of nothing in particular, while you sweep your hands through the air in front of you, palms parallel to the ground. Alternatively, you may be able to sense shifts and differences in the energy of an area by holding your palms upright and facing away from you.

When you feel you've found a spirit road of some sort, visit it often and get to know it throughout the seasons. As areas of special power in a landscape, they are good places to perform divination, journeying, and spellwork. They are also good for befriending the local spirits over time, as well as earth healing, depending on what type of energy you feel there.

Give Back to the Land

Make friends with the natural spirits of your area, whatever they may be. Rekindle the tradition of offerings—of song, water or wine, or a bowl of butter. Some sacred herbs, a pinch of tobacco, a sprinkle of cedar, or a whole homecooked meal…what are the traditions of your land? If you go still and listen, what do the quiet voices of the spirits say to you, as soft as a breeze on your cheek? Mugwort (*Artemisia vulgaris*) and vervain (*Verbena officinalis*) are helpful, I find. This land knows them, and they tell the land that I remember it is holy. Burning these as incense or smudge sticks purifies the space, and mugwort in particular helps develop the second sight—so it helps communication all around. I grow them myself, with great care and love, and thank my plant friends for their work. I find that gifts of ochre and butter are beloved by ancestral spirits. I bring fresh spring water to trees and plant spirits, gifts of song to rivers and the faery folk, gossip to the bees, and oat cakes to storms. With the gifts, the offerings, comes a ritual exchange. If you show your respect, they will respect you in return, though not always straightaway, so be patient and strong—you may be challenged. There may be work to do; it won't always be easy, but your relationship has begun.

A Circle of Friends

No wise Witch ever works alone. Though she may need no coven, and sisters may be spread far and wide, the very earth itself calls her daughter. She belongs to the land. The green fields are her mantle, the sky her eyes. The trees are her brothers and the hillside her treasure chest. Her soul is the land and her heart is its fireside. A wisewoman's magic can be a small thing, but it floats on the wind beyond all horizons. A wise Witch reads the patterns of autumn leaves in the lane and flickering flames. Her spells are sung in birdsong and falling rain, and are as strong as weeds and oak trees and as sure as spring.

Danu Forest *has been a practicing Witch and wisewoman in the Celtic tradition for over 25 years, and has been teaching for over a decade. Living in Glastonbury in the rural south west of Britain, she is an Ard Bandrui (Arch Druidess) with the Druid Clan of Dana and runs her own group, The Grove of the Avalon Sidhe, as well as holding regular trainings, online courses, ceremonies and private consultations. She is widely published and is the author of several books, including* Nature Spirits, The Druid Shaman, Celtic Tree Magic, *and* The Magical Year. *For more information, visit www.danuforest.co.uk.*

Illustrator: Tim Foley

"What Are You?" A Journey of Spiritual Identity

Natalie Zaman

Priestess Miriam Chamani sits across from me and smiles. "So tell me. What brought you to this table?"

I had gone to New Orleans because I love it and because, unconsciously, something inside me needed to be shaken up—it happens every time I go there.

Despite the relative coolness of the Voodoo Spiritual Temple, I'm sweating—and not because of the Louisiana summer heat. At last, I'm getting the African bone reading I've always wanted. On all of my prior trips, Priestess Miriam was

either out or booked up—but the third time's the charm. In hindsight, I can safely say that I probably wasn't ready for it earlier.

"People like to be lied to," she says. Her voice is sing-song chanty, and she laughs before digging a little deeper. "What are you running from?"

I stare at the table littered with bones that look like amber, stones, and fragments of cowrie shells, tongue-tied. Then something inside rattles loose the true purpose of this visit. Not divination but a look in the mirror, and I know she can see this.

"You're not gonna be of much use if you're all over the place," she tells me.

This isn't my first encounter with Priestess Miriam. I'd visited the Voodoo Spiritual Temple years before and was dazzled by it. Even though I didn't get a reading, she had a message for me then, too. The same one she was telling me now.

"You've got to float."

I'm guessing she didn't mean float "away." I'd been floating—at least, I thought I'd been, traveling from place to place, discovering, becoming enlightened, and collecting things. My "office" is filled with veladoras, crystal skulls, wands, books and more books, wizard ponies, unicorns, dragons, a Thai spirit house, and representations of those spirits and deities whom I feel are my guides: Gaia, Ganesha, Budai, and Marie Laveau. It's my sacred space, and I've filled it with travel treasures that I want to be talismans but are more like souvenirs.

Back in the Voodoo Spiritual Temple, Priestess Miriam stares at me, I hope, sympathetically. "There are days I'd rather be anywhere but here," she tells me, more softly. "But if I'd only listened to myself and not to God, well, we wouldn't be sitting right here, right now."

I have a bad habit of only hearing my own voice when I get passionate about something. Traveling has never failed to bring me new and different things to love. Every journey brings some kind of enlightenment or fresh revelation, some of which have tantalizing hints of familiarity—and so far, that's been enough. But really, it isn't, because it's hard to be focused when you're always moving. It's difficult to establish a meaningful, comforting, and effective means of prayer, ritual, worship—whatever you want to call it—when everything is always new. It's hard to be whole when you don't take the time to delve deeply.

I'd once had roots, and I was realizing that I missed them.

Losing My Way

Spirituality is an anchor that grounds you but doesn't weigh you down. Through its lens, life makes sense and the unendurable becomes endurable. You float, but there is something bigger than you holding you up. I was raised Catholic. I went to Catholic grammar school, Catholic high school (for two years), and after that, Catholic college by my own choice. I found great comfort in this faith. It was so dependable: a saint for every trouble, a prayer to ease any ill, and an answer to every question, even if that answer was "just believe."

I remember the day all that came to an end for me. I was sitting in a classroom at Rutgers University at an art history lecture on Byzantine tomb paintings. The professor put up a slide of the god Apollo, easily recognizable with his laurel wreath and blond hair.

"Here," I can still hear her saying, "we have an early representation of Christ."

Excuse me?

That was a Greek god. He was make-believe, not real like the Jesus I knew—the gentle-eyed, bearded, ageless father figure who had always been a part of my life, albeit dimly sometimes.

But she went on to relentlessly, mercilessly, illustrate the evolution of the image of Jesus, and with every word, I felt sick. However I'd been brought up in terms of religion, this was *history*. And in that awful moment I realized that if what I was hearing was true, then just about everything I'd been taught since childhood *was a lie*. All reason, redemption, and everything that had been laid out so simply for so long was now out of my reach. I didn't have the answers anymore—they were somewhere "out there," and I was free to try to find them. Freedom, I discovered, can be

I didn't have the answers anymore—they were somewhere "out there," and I was free to try to find them. Freedom, I discovered, can be just as terrifying as it is exhilarating, especially when you don't plan for it.

just as terrifying as it is exhilarating, especially when you don't plan for it. So I did the only thing I knew how to do: I read.

I read the suppressed and edited books of the Bible. Fear turned to anger at this discovery—who *edits* God? Factual biographies of my beloved saints showed them to be just as human as holy. But despite the confirmation and reconfirmation of what I was learning, I found it difficult to turn my back on what had been instilled in me pretty much since birth. Events brought me back to church. When my children were born, and on 9/11 (my husband was at the World Trade Center that day), I came back, the prodigal daughter, always welcomed but never quite feeling at home anymore. I would look up at crucifixes and statues and wonder, *What's your real story?* It was no longer enough for me to "just believe."

The gods (and goddesses) set me on this path, so I followed them—and found Celtic Wicca. I loved learning the origins of the holidays I'd celebrated my whole life, elemental workings, tracing the paths of the moon and the stars, and getting to know the cycle of the seasons more intimately. This incarnation of the Craft doesn't have a monopoly on these things, but there was another, more intimate reason this path appealed to me. My mom is Italian, and I grew up surrounded by her family. I never really knew anything about my dad's side, except that they were Scottish, with some Welsh, English, and a bit of French thrown in. I don't even remember him mentioning any siblings (he had two sisters and a brother). When he left the family when I was ten, it was like he and everything about him were out of my life forever. Through this path I'd found a means of connecting with my unknown ancestors, one of whom—my dad's eldest sister—I resembled so closely that a childhood friend of his who crossed our paths one day stopped my mother to ask her "if I was a Davidson." Had I finally found my place?

If only.

As I continued my studies, cracks began to form in the connection I'd felt so strongly when I started. I think the biggest thing was that I wasn't Irish. My elder was, and our work was heavily focused there. I felt closer to British and Norse traditions. I also found myself drawn to aspects of other religions—Budai, the jolly laughing Buddha; Voodoo veves; the kind eyes of Ganesha; and Marie Laveau, whose life read like a saint's to me. And there were elements of Catholicism I didn't want to abandon, even though a part of me still felt betrayed: candles and incense, the Blessed Mother and Saint Francis, music and angels. Through them I connected to countless ancestors and to family who still believed. Did I belong anywhere? *What was I?*

Not All Those Who Wander Are Lost

After the bone reading, I make my way back across the French Quarter to the Cathedral Basilica of Saint Louis, with a lot to think about.

"When you're grounded, you won't be so scattered," Priestess Miriam had told me.

The square in front of the cathedral is lined with artists and palm and card readers and swells with the sound of drumbeats and brass—but inside, all is quiet. Both places are equally sacred. I sit in a pew in the back row, remembering that Marie Laveau was comfortable with feet in two worlds: here in this cathedral and dancing only blocks away in Congo Square. My roots have spread, but I've not tended them—and I know what the next leg of my journey must be:

Studying.

Questioning.

Practicing.

Healing.

Revisiting—places, people, ritual.

And just believing.

I must learn as much as I can, try to understand the why and how of these connections and acknowledge their origins. It may take a lifetime. Luckily, I know a really good and simple grounding ritual. Closing my eyes, I breathe deeply, taking in the scent of incense and candles—familiar, comfortable smells. I slip the St. Christopher medal out of my pocket and whisper, "Patron of travelers, walk with me."

I am welcomed home again, this time with the knowledge that I'll always be a pilgrim.

. . . .

In February of 2016, the Voodoo Spiritual Temple in New Orleans suffered a devastating fire. Efforts are being made to relocate, restore, and rebuild this sacred space. For more information, see http://wild hunt.org/2016/02/fire-destroys-historic-home-of-new-orleans -voodoo-spiritual-temple.html.

Natalie Zaman *is a regular contributor to various Llewellyn annuals. She is the author of the upcoming* Magical Destinations of the North- east (Llewellyn, 2016) *and writes the recurring feature* "Wandering Witch" *for* Witches & Pagans *magazine. Her work has also appeared in* FATE, SageWoman, *and* newWitch *magazines. When she's not on the road, she's chasing free-range hens in her self-sufficient and Pagan-friendly back garden. Find Natalie online at http://nataliezaman.blogspot.com.*

Illustrator: Kathleen Edwards

The Art of Letting Go

Shawna Galvin

Letting go is part of the human condition. It's an opportunity for healing and growth as we learn from, and move away from, those things we need to let go of. It's a lifelong journey.

Various stages of life bring many different things people often want to let go of, including past regrets, negative energy, fear, anger, and toxic relationships.

Past regrets might include wishing we hadn't done a certain thing, or wishing we could go back and handle something in a different way. I still shudder at things my mother went through while in the hospital with cancer from October 2003 to the end of that December when she passed away. I was her advocate and did the best I could. Looking back, I wish there were things I could go back and change, such as simply getting the doctors to communicate with each other during  the last two months of her life. I wish I knew then what I know now, but experience is part of our life lessons. Over time, I've come to remember my mother as she was before the cancer, and even appreciate the time we had together while sitting together at her chemotherapy appointments.

I was six months pregnant with her first grandchild when my mother passed away, and although it was sad, in a way, Mom got to know her grandson before he was born. Now I see so much of my mother in my son, especially her wit and many of her gestures. This brings me joy. Grief comes in waves, and everyone deals with it differently. We don't want to let go of our friends and loved ones when they cross over. It's not really "letting go" in the sense of forgetting, but is perhaps gaining new a perspective on death, loss, and the mystery of life. Letting go of my mother wasn't easy. I miss her every day, but I see her through my son, which is a beautiful thing.

Also, there are things we regret doing, and that has a lot to do with forgiving ourselves. Even if we can't fully forgive ourselves, we need to face the pain now and then, and this means getting help if it gets too deep.

Protection from Fear and Negativity

In all my years of studying energy and healing with other spiritual healers, the greatest gifts they gave to me were the tools for protection. This doesn't mean I'm immune to any sort of negative energy; it just means I feel more prepared and knowledgeable about using protection. I was raised Catholic, so I learned prayer as a means of protection at a young age. As I grew up, I continued to explore my own spirituality and work with healers. I became a Reiki II practitioner. I also had polarity energy treatments and a few spiritual readings, studied and practiced meditation, and delved into homeopathic remedies.

Most of these practices begin and end with visualizing a white or other colored light going through our bodies and throughout the work space. Crystals, incense, and white sage smoke are used for clearing rooms, clearing ourselves, and creating a positive environment,

along with calling on positive energy and not allowing negative energy in. Breathing techniques are also used. I have been using these things automatically in my life.

I say the "Hail Mary" often as a prayer and personal mantra to give me strength and pull me through hard times and also because I enjoy saying it to myself, using the purple light of St. Germain, as was taught to me by my late spiritual reader. She told me to visualize the purple flame within me and say something like, "I am the purple flame of St. Germain. I guard you from the north, south, east, west, and from the center where everything comes from." I use this for extra protection.

The way I visualize white light or another brightly colored light, such as pink or blue, is to see it surrounding my body and imagine it entering through the top of my head, flowing throughout all of my limbs, and shooting out through my fingertips and toes. Filling ourselves with light through visualization is both a clearing and a grounding experience, along with taking some slow cleansing breaths. I do these practices when I'm in my car, flying in a plane, going to work, or just lying in bed at night. I also visualize healing light around my loved ones.

Smudging with white sage has become a favorite technique of mine for clearing out negativity. I smudge with white sage when moving into a new house or whenever I feel our house is ready for a clearing. I burn the end of my bundle of white sage and walk around to each room as the smoke flows to the corners of each space. I also do this if something negative enters our life: a negative situation, a negative person, illness, or when it all just feels like too much.

I have collected rocks from a very young age. Later on, I learned more about crystals from my healers and on my own, and took this further by studying geology in college. To this day, I keep rocks and stones around me, ones that I am drawn to and that I like, and also stones with certain healing properties. I tend to wear moonstone often to keep negativity at bay as much as possible and let positive energy in. Other stones I'm drawn to for healing energy include quartz crystal, amethyst, Herkimer diamond, London blue topaz, and lapis.

Techniques to Help You Let Go

Here are some techniques that help me let go. Perhaps you will use some of these techniques or find and practice what feels good for you.

Breathe. Take a slow, deep breath in through your nose, hold that breath for a few seconds, then breathe out slowly through your mouth, letting all the air out. Repeat a few times. This will really help you focus on the moment and regroup.

Surround yourself with healing energy, such as white light. Visualize this going through you, cocooning you, energizing you, and bathing you in love.

Getting up and moving around helps. Throw yourself a private dance party, mow the lawn, work in the garden, swim, jump the ocean waves, hike, or sled. Whatever gets you up and about can help.

Nature especially is something I'm drawn to when I need to just be at peace. It gives me a sense of being at one with Spirit. I am drawn to the ocean in particular, in any sort of weather, at any time of day. Perhaps it's the constant change of the ocean I love combined with the scent of it, the air, and the exhilarating feeling I get from being by the sea. Other things I love anywhere are stargazing, sunsets, clouds, flowers, trees, plant life, rocks, mountains, lakes, rivers, streams, or any natural body of water.

Indoors (and even outdoors sometimes, weather permitting), I love to read, write, listen to music, and talk with family and friends. Going to see art at museums is something that uplifts me. There is so much beauty and joy in life.

It helps to change your thoughts in order to make major changes. Try to make a plan, or have a plan in place, and get some support. Some changes take longer than others, and some situations require outside help and resources.

Take time to concentrate on you, no matter what sort of a busy day you have. Schedule some time just for you. Even just stepping outside and taking deep breaths, looking at the sky, and appreciating the moment can be rejuvenating.

Full moons are a good time for releasing things, especially the Flower Moon in May, although any full moon will work. The full moon is a time when we often have the most energy and heightened senses, and is perhaps when we feel closer to spiritual entities. This is a good time to gain or end something and banish negativity. There are a variety of full moon rituals designed to help you let go of the past and clear out negative energy. I simply go outside, even if just for a minute, and bathe in the moonlight. I also try to do some writing. This is a time when my dreams frequently give me some creative ideas for writing my poetry, short stories, and novels. I'm no artist, but I have painted watercolors over the years inspired by dreams; these I keep to myself.

Wanting to make changes in life takes work. I'm on a path where I am exercising more and eating better. For me, I have to really want something, commit to it, and, most of all, work at it. I have to accept that sometimes I will get off-track, too.

. . . .

The moment you want to move on, the moment you are willing to change and release, you begin to let go.

Letting go can feel incredible, but it can also require a lot of work. Breathe; surround yourself with healing energy and clear out negative energy.

Take each day one step at a time. You might go backward some days, but try to remember why you started, and get back to the positive.

Shawna Galvin *lives in Maine and earned a Master of Fine Arts in Creative Writing at the University of Southern Maine Stonecoast inaugural class of 2004. Her novel,* The Ghost in You, *was released in 2014, and a collection of poetry and essays,* Mimi's Alchemy: A Grandmother's Magic, *was released in February 2014. Shawna's short stories, articles, flash fiction, and poetry have appeared in publications such as* Words & Images *and USM's* Free Press. *She has edited short stories for* Brutal as Hell, *is a freelance editor, and has embarked on a spooky publishing journey at Macabre Maine while continuing to write. Visit her at shawnagalvin.com and http://macabremaine.wix.com/macabremaine.*

Illustrator: Jennifer Hewitson

The Lunar Calendar

September 2016 to December 2017

SEPTEMBER

S	M	T	W	T	F	S
				1	2	3
4	5	6	7	8	9	10
11	12	13	14	15	16	17
18	19	20	21	22	23	24
25	26	27	28	29	30	

OCTOBER

S	M	T	W	T	F	S
						1
2	3	4	5	6	7	8
9	10	11	12	13	14	15
16	17	18	19	20	21	22
23	24	25	26	27	28	29
30	31					

NOVEMBER

S	M	T	W	T	F	S
		1	2	3	4	5
6	7	8	9	10	11	12
13	14	15	16	17	18	19
20	21	22	23	24	25	26
27	28	29	30			

DECEMBER

S	M	T	W	T	F	S
				1	2	3
4	5	6	7	8	9	10
11	12	13	14	15	16	17
18	19	20	21	22	23	24
25	26	27	28	29	30	31

2017

JANUARY

S	M	T	W	T	F	S
1	2	3	4	5	6	7
8	9	10	11	12	13	14
15	16	17	18	19	20	21
22	23	24	25	26	27	28
29	30	31				

FEBRUARY

S	M	T	W	T	F	S
			1	2	3	4
5	6	7	8	9	10	11
12	13	14	15	16	17	18
19	20	21	22	23	24	25
26	27	28				

MARCH

S	M	T	W	T	F	S
			1	2	3	4
5	6	7	8	9	10	11
12	13	14	15	16	17	18
19	20	21	22	23	24	25
26	27	28	29	30	31	

APRIL

S	M	T	W	T	F	S
						1
2	3	4	5	6	7	8
9	10	11	12	13	14	15
16	17	18	19	20	21	22
23	24	25	26	27	28	29
30						

MAY

S	M	T	W	T	F	S
	1	2	3	4	5	6
7	8	9	10	11	12	13
14	15	16	17	18	19	20
21	22	23	24	25	26	27
28	29	30	31			

JUNE

S	M	T	W	T	F	S
				1	2	3
4	5	6	7	8	9	10
11	12	13	14	15	16	17
18	19	20	21	22	23	24
25	26	27	28	29	30	

JULY

S	M	T	W	T	F	S
						1
2	3	4	5	6	7	8
9	10	11	12	13	14	15
16	17	18	19	20	21	22
23	24	25	26	27	28	29
30	31					

AUGUST

S	M	T	W	T	F	S
		1	2	3	4	5
6	7	8	9	10	11	12
13	14	15	16	17	18	19
20	21	22	23	24	25	26
27	28	29	30	31		

SEPTEMBER

S	M	T	W	T	F	S
					1	2
3	4	5	6	7	8	9
10	11	12	13	14	15	16
17	18	19	20	21	22	23
24	25	26	27	28	29	30

OCTOBER

S	M	T	W	T	F	S
1	2	3	4	5	6	7
8	9	10	11	12	13	14
15	16	17	18	19	20	21
22	23	24	25	26	27	28
29	30	31				

NOVEMBER

S	M	T	W	T	F	S
			1	2	3	4
5	6	7	8	9	10	11
12	13	14	15	16	17	18
19	20	21	22	23	24	25
26	27	28	29	30		

DECEMBER

S	M	T	W	T	F	S
					1	2
3	4	5	6	7	8	9
10	11	12	13	14	15	16
17	18	19	20	21	22	23
24	25	26	27	28	29	30
31						

2016
SEPTEMBER

SU	M	TU	W	TH	F	SA
				1 ● Solar Eclipse, New Moon 5:03 am	2	3
4	5 Labor Day	6	7	8	9	10
11	12	13	14	15	16 ☺ Lunar Eclipse, Harvest Moon 3:05 pm	17
18	19	20	21	22 Mabon/ Fall Equinox	23	24
25	26	27	28	29	30 ● New Moon 8:11 pm	

Times are in Eastern Time.

SU	M	TU	W	TH	F	SA
						1
2	3	4	5	6	7	8
9	10	11	12	13	14	15
16 ☺ Blood Moon 12:23 am	17	18	19	20	21	22
23	24	25	26	27	28	29
30 ● New Moon 1:38 pm	31 *Samhain/* *Halloween*					

Times are in Eastern Time.

2016
NOVEMBER

SU	M	TU	W	TH	F	SA
		1 All Saints' Day	2	3	4	5
6 DST *ends 2 am*	7	8 Election Day (general)	9	10	11	12
13	14 ☺ Mourning Moon, 8:52 am	15	16	17	18	19
20	21	22	23	24 Thanksgiving Day	25	26
27	28	29 ● New Moon 7:18 am	30			

Times are in Eastern Time.

2016
DECEMBER

SU	M	TU	W	TH	F	SA
				1	2	3
4	5	6	7	8	9	10
11	12	13 ☺ Long Nights Moon 7:06 pm	14	15	16	17
18	19	20	21 Yule/ Winter Solstice	22	23	24 Christmas Eve
25 Christmas Day	26	27	28	29 ● New Moon 1:53 am	30	31 New Year's Eve

Times are in Eastern Time.

2017
JANUARY

SU	M	TU	W	TH	F	SA
1 *New Year's Day*	2	3	4	5	6	7
8	9	10	11	12 ☺ Cold Moon 6:34 am	13	14
15	16 *Martin Luther King, Jr. Day*	17	18	19	20	21
22	23	24	25	26	27 ● New Moon 7:07 pm	28
29	30	31				

Times are in Eastern Time.

2017
FEBRUARY

SU	M	TU	W	TH	F	SA
			1	2 *Imbolc/ Groundhog Day*	3	4
5	6	7	8	9	10 ☺ Lunar Eclipse, Quickening Moon , 7:33 pm	11
12	13	14	15	16	17	18
19	20 *Presidents' Day*	21	22	23	24	25
26 ● Solar Eclipse, New Moon 9:58 am	27	28				

Times are in Eastern Time.

2017
MARCH

SU	M	TU	W	TH	F	SA
			I	2	3	4
5	6	7	8	9	10	II
I2 ☻ Storm Moon 10:54 am DST *begins 2 am*	I3	I4	I5	I6	I7 *St. Patrick's Day*	I8
I9	20 *Ostara/ Spring Equinox*	2I	22	23	24	25
26	27 ● New Moon 10:57 pm	28	29	30	3I	

Times are in Eastern Time.

2017
APRIL

SU	M	TU	W	TH	F	SA
						1
						All Fools' Day
2	3	4	5	6	7	8
9	10	11 ☺	12	13	14	15
		Wind Moon 2:08 am				
16	17	18	19	20	21	22
						Earth Day
23	24	25	26 ●	27	28	29
			New Moon 8:16 am			
30						

Times are in Eastern Time.

2017
MAY

SU	M	TU	W	TH	F	SA
	1	2	3	4	5	6
	Beltane					
7	8	9	10 ☺	11	12	13
			Flower Moon 5:42 pm			
14	15	16	17	18	19	20
Mother's Day						
21	22	23	24	25 ●	26	27
				New Moon 3:44 pm		
28	29	30	31			
	Memorial Day					

Times are in Eastern Time.

2017
JUNE

SU	M	TU	W	TH	F	SA
				1	2	3
4	5	6	7	8	9 ☺ Strong Sun Moon 9:10 am	10
11	12	13	14 *Flag Day*	15	16	17
18 *Father's Day*	19	20	21 *Litha/ Summer Solstice*	22	23 ● New Moon 10:31 pm	24
25	26	27	28	29	30	

Times are in Eastern Time.

2017
JULY

SU	M	TU	W	TH	F	SA
						1
2	3	4 *Independence Day*	5	6	7	8
9 ☺ Blessing Moon 12:07 am	10	11	12	13	14	15
16	17	18	19	20	21	22
23 ● New Moon 5:46 am	24	25	26	27	28	29
30	31					

Times are in Eastern Time.

2017
AUGUST

SU	M	TU	W	TH	F	SA
		1 *Lammas*	2	3	4	5
6	7 ☺ Lunar Eclipse, Corn Moon 2:11 pm	8	9	10	11	12
13	14	15	16	17	18	19
20	21 ● Solar Eclipse, New Moon 2:30 pm	22	23	24	25	26
27	28	29	30	31		

Times are in Eastern Time.

2017
SEPTEMBER

SU	M	TU	W	TH	F	SA
					1	2
3	4 *Labor Day*	5	6 ☺ Harvest Moon 3:03 am	7	8	9
10	11	12	13	14	15	16
17	18	19	20 ● New Moon 1:30 am	21	22 *Mabon/ Fall Equinox*	23
24	25	26	27	28	29	30

Times are in Eastern Time.

2017
OCTOBER

SU	M	TU	W	TH	F	SA
1	2	3	4	5 ☺ Blood Moon 2:40 pm	6	7
8	9	10	11	12	13	14
15	16	17	18	19 ● New Moon 3:12 pm	20	21
22	23	24	25	26	27	28
29	30	31 *Samhain/* *Halloween*				

Times are in Eastern Time.

2017
NOVEMBER

SU	M	TU	W	TH	F	SA
			1 *All Saints' Day*	2	3	4 ☺ Mourning Moon, 1:23 am
5 *DST ends 2 am*	6	7 *Election Day* *(general)*	8	9	10	11
12	13	14	15	16	17	18 ● New Moon 6:42 am
19	20	21	22	23 *Thanksgiving* *Day*	24	25
26	27	28	29	30		

Times are in Eastern Time.

2017
DECEMBER

SU	M	TU	W	TH	F	SA
					1	2
3 ☺ Long Nights Moon 10:47 am	4	5	6	7	8	9
10	11	12	13	14	15	16
17	18 ● New Moon 1:30 am	19	20	21 Yule/ Winter Solstice	22	23
24 *Christmas Eve*	25 *Christmas Day*	26	27	28	29	30
31 *New Year's Eve*						

Times are in Eastern Time.

GET MORE AT LLEWELLYN.COM

Visit us online to browse hundreds of our books and decks, plus sign up to receive our e-newsletters and exclusive online offers.

- **Free tarot readings • Spell-A-Day • Moon phases**
- **Recipes, spells, and tips • Blogs • Encyclopedia**
- **Author interviews, articles, and upcoming events**

GET SOCIAL WITH LLEWELLYN

Find us on Facebook

www.Facebook.com/LlewellynBooks

Follow us on twitter™

www.Twitter.com/Llewellynbooks

GET BOOKS AT LLEWELLYN

LLEWELLYN ORDERING INFORMATION

Order online: Visit our website at www.llewellyn.com to select your books and place an order on our secure server.

Order by phone:
- Call toll free within the U.S. at 1-877-NEW-WRLD (1-877-639-9753)
- Call toll free within Canada at 1-866-NEW-WRLD (1-866-639-9753)
- We accept VISA, MasterCard, American Express and Discover

Order by mail:
Send the full price of your order (MN residents add 6.875% sales tax) in U.S. funds, plus postage and handling to: Llewellyn Worldwide, 2143 Wooddale Drive Woodbury, MN 55125-2989

POSTAGE AND HANDLING

STANDARD (U.S. & Canada):
(Please allow 12 business days)
$30.00 and under, add $4.00.
$30.01 and over, FREE SHIPPING.

INTERNATIONAL ORDERS:
$16.00 for one book, plus $3.00 for each additional book.

Visit us online for more shipping options. Prices subject to change.

FREE CATALOG!

To order, call
1-877-
NEW-WRLD
ext. 8236
or visit our
website